D0220955

The life of Schubert

Musical lives

Each book in this series describes the life
and music of a major composer, revealing
the private as well as the public figure. While
the main thread is biographical, the music
appears as an integral part of the narrative,
each volume thus presenting an organic view
of the composer, the music and the circumstances in which the music was written.

Published titles

The life of Schubert

CHRISTOPHER H. GIBBS

CAMBRIDGE
UNIVERSITY PRESS

PUBLISHED BY THE PRESS SYNDICATE OF THE UNIVERSITY OF CAMBRIDGE
The Pitt Building, Trumpington Street, Cambridge, United Kingdom

CAMBRIDGE UNIVERSITY PRESS
The Edinburgh Building, Cambridge CB2 2RU, UK
40 West 20th Street, New York, NY 10011–4211, USA
10 Stamford Road, Oakleigh, VIC 3166, Australia
Ruiz de Alarcón 13, 28014 Madrid, Spain
Dock House, The Waterfront, Cape Town 8001, South Africa

http://www.cambridge.org

First published 2000, Reprinted 2000

Printed in the United Kingdom at the University Press, Cambridge

Typeset in FF Quadraat 9.75/14 pt, in QuarkXPress™ [SE]

A catalogue record for this book is available from the British Library

Library of Congress cataloguing in publication data

Gibbs, Christopher Howard.
    The life of Schubert / Christopher H. Gibbs.
        p.   cm. – (Musical lives)
    Includes bibliographical references and index.
    ISBN 0 521 59426 X
        1. Schubert, Franz, 1797–1828.   2. Composers – Austria Biography.
    I. Title.   II. Series.
ML410.S3G53   2000   780′.92 – dc21   [B]   99-32936 CIP

ISBN 0 521 59426 X   hardback
ISBN 0 521 59512 6   paperback

for Howard and Janet Gibbs

Contents

ILLUSTRATIONS

Grateful acknowledgement is due for the use of illustrations from the following sources: Carolinen-Sammlung, Vienna (3,4,5,6,9,14); Historisches Museum der Stadt Wien (8,10,11); Sammlungen der

Gesellschaft der Musikfreunde in Wien (17); Wiener Stadt- und
Landesbibliothek, Musiksammlung (18); International Franz
Schubert Institute (12,16); Beethoven-Haus, Bonn (15); Albertina,
Graphische Sammlung (1); author's collection (19,20); and
reproductions from *Die historischen Bildnisse Franz Schuberts in getreuen
Nachbildungen*, ed. Otto Erich Deutsch (Vienna, 1922) (2,13).

ACKNOWLEDGMENTS

Some of the ideas explored in this biography were first broached a decade ago in my dissertation at Columbia University, and I am indebted to Professors Edward A. Lippman, Walter Frisch, and Ian Bent for their initial support. My immersion in Schubert's music continued as I participated in the Schubertiade Festival at the 92nd Street Y in New York City. I would like to express my gratitude to that institution, and to Trudy Miller, Omus Hirshbein, and Joseph Horowitz, and the late Hermann Prey for the opportunities they offered. The Schubertiade sent me to Vienna each summer, where I received assistance from the Gesellschaft der Musikfreunde; the Stadt- und Landesbibliothek, Musiksammlung; and the Österreichische Nationalbibliothek, Musiksammlung. Ernst Hilmar, general secretary of the International Franz Schubert Institute, has given particularly valuable aid.

Initial research for this project was aided by grants from the Österreichisches Bundesministerium für Wissenschaft und Forschung, the Lane Cooper Fellowship, administered by the New York Charitable Trust, and the Austrian Cultural Institute. I gratefully acknowledge as well the Julian Park Publication Fund at the State University of New York at Buffalo for supporting the cost of some of the illustrations. I would also like to thank Penny Souster, music editor at Cambridge University Press, for suggesting that I write this biography and for her patient encouragement throughout.

Colleagues who have read earlier versions of parts or all of this book have corrected errors, helped to refine its arguments, and challenged some of my interpretations. Michael Lorenz generously offered suggestions and searched Vienna's archives to elucidate various factual matters. Two good friends in Vienna, Morten Solvik and Robert O. de Clercq, gave first readings that immeasurably helped me to focus the core issues. The latter also generously provided many of the illustrations drawn from the Carolinen-Sammlung, of which he is curator. His elegant new translation of Schubert's poem "Mein Gebet" appears on page 108.

Christopher Hatch continues to review much of my published prose with patience, understanding, and unobtrusive guidance. Likewise, Donald Wilson, who first introduced me to Schubert's music in high school, read a late version of the manuscript with keen discernment. I am grateful to these ideal readers for their ongoing friendship, encouragement, and teaching. My final personal thanks are to my wife Helena Sedláčková Gibbs, whose literary, psycho-analytic, and critical perspectives continually enlarge and enrich my intellectual horizons, and to my all-so-supportive parents, Howard and Janet Gibbs, to whom this effort is lovingly dedicated.

Otto Erich Deutsch's two essential collections of documents relating to Schubert's life are cited within the body of this book using the abbreviations given below. While in general I have tried to keep intrusive references to a minimum, it is important, especially given the current heated debates about Schubert, that quotations be identified so that interested readers are able to check the complete context and, with a bit more industry, to locate the original German text. (I have often modified or re-translated the cited English-language editions.) When the citation is not given for a quotation it is because the source can be located by the date. I beg the reader's patience for including these important internal references.

Concerning "Deutsch Numbers": Deutsch himself felt that it was unnecessary for the catalogue numbers he devised to be provided for every song, opera, and so forth, but rather that they should be used primarily to distinguish instrumental compositions. Although the numbers generally run chronologically – i.e. D114 is relatively early, while D960 is very late – this is often misleading as advances in dating methods have recast the chronology of many works. For these reasons, I have not included Deutsch numbers for vocal compositions unless there might otherwise be some cause for confusion.

SDB   *Schubert: A Documentary Biography.* Trans. Eric Blom. London, 1946. (The American edition is entitled *The Schubert Reader: A Life of Franz Schubert in Letters and Documents* [New York, 1947].)

SMF   *Schubert: Memoirs by his Friends.* Trans. Rosamond Ley and John Nowell. London, 1958.

Prologue: Schubert yesterday

This book concerns less *The Life of Schubert* than "The Life of Schubert's Career," a story more of the artist than the man. Perhaps someday a trove of new material will surface that might allow a future historian to write an intimate portrait of the man and artist, the son, brother, and friend. But for now, and probably forever, scholars can only speculate about such fundamental matters as Schubert's relations with his parents (his mother is virtually missing from all the surviving evidence) or about the true nature of his romantic and sexual activities. A recurring theme of this brief biography will be the reasons for, and the consequences of, voids in documenting Schubert's life, absences that have been filled with much fantasy and many projected images created by others, whether in popular biographies, novels, operettas, or movies.

The most important scholarly work on the composer in recent decades – including the German version of Otto Erich Deutsch's catalogue of compositions, a new complete edition of the music, and sophisticated critical and analytical studies – allows the full breadth of Schubert's creative achievement to shine forth as never before. Even though technical accounts are beyond the scope of this series of Musical Lives, some general musical observations are provided in relation to Schubert's professional career. The discussions of the music herein gain in length and significance as the composer matures, with special emphasis on his late compositions. My primary concern is to appreciate how Schubert negotiated between intimate songs, dances, and keyboard miniatures, and his far more ambitious instrumental, dramatic, and sacred projects.

The introductory chapter examines three visual depictions of Schubert (and can be read later if one wants to plunge immediately into the life story in chapter 2), and those that follow are roughly chronological, with each concentrating on larger issues relevant to the composer's daily existence, music, and reputation. Chapter titles are intended to capture the changes in Schubert's life, as well as some of the clichés about that life. I place particular importance on the social and musical culture in which Schubert lived and worked in Vienna, and on the friends who played such a large role in his aesthetic education, in his everyday activities, and in the construction of his image. The last chapter charts Schubert's "life" after his premature death, for if his physical body expired at age thirty-one, his body of work flourished as unknown compositions continued to be discovered, and as his legacy was constantly reassessed. The posthumous "Life of Schubert's Career" spans the nineteenth century – and beyond.

In keeping with an overriding concern for Schubert's compositional and professional development, I focus specifically on his relationship to Beethoven – not so much on any personal contact between them, or even on what Schubert learned compositionally from the older master (albeit indirectly), as on how Beethoven served as his essential professional model and later became the touchstone – explicit and implicit – for discussions of Schubert's life and works. My identification of a "secret program" to the late Piano Trio in E flat, Op. 100 (D929), provides significant new evidence of Beethoven's importance. Schubert could not, nor did he wish to, escape Beethoven's example and legacy.

In the end, my view of Schubert's professional life is optimistic, perhaps at times even overcompensating for the historically pervasive images of a "poor Schubert" – without money, love, fame, or good health. I aim to counter the idea of the neglected Schubert by empowering him with responsibility for his life and works. I believe it is possible to reconcile the undivided accounts of Schubert's timid, humble, and often childlike nature with evidence of a fierce awareness of his artistic genius and worth. For too long, his shyness has been confused with low self-esteem and lack of self-confidence. My approach is affirmative because it directs appropriate attention on the successes of Schubert's budding career, and not, as is usually the case, on an occasional bad review, troubles with certain publishers, or rejections from jobs he probably did not want anyway. No doubt some phases in his short creative life were extremely frustrating and discouraging, but Schubert proved remarkably adaptive. For nearly two centuries commentators have lamented his early death because it robbed posterity of further masterpieces; we might flip this formulation around and say that Schubert was personally robbed of the hardearned success he was finally winning by the end of the 1820s.

In certain respects this book aims to be an "anti-biography." I shall emphasize the distortion and trivialization of his life that formed and informed popular images. Such an approach does not pretend to present definitively the "true" man and composer, but rather seeks to recount what can be reliably documented and to examine some of the most persistent legends. But no matter how current the scholarship and critical the examination, constructing a narrative of Schubert's life, be it during the nineteenth century or now at the turn of the millennium, necessarily reflects contemporaneous interpretations, concerns, and methods, and constitutes Schubert's subjectivity according to contemporaneous theories, paradigms, and cultural context. While examining Schubert's place in history, any reconsideration will itself be part of that history. This is the necessity, as well as the value, of retelling Schubert's story.

In the closing years of the twentieth century a new Schubert image has suddenly emerged, generating considerable controversy. The explorations of Schubert's possible homosexuality, depression, habitual drinking, and neuroses have all made for alluring headlines and are a striking counter-pole to the trivial image of the guileless

"Prince of Song" that had reigned for so long. There is often also, I believe, a great deal more truth to the revised view. And yet we are currently at a point where some unproven claims about the darker Schubert threaten to become a new orthodoxy in the absence of sufficient historical investigation or evidence. Ultimately, Schubert remains elusive. It is my hope that this book dispels some of the sentimental platitudes of the past, gives a better idea of the conditions that formed Schubert's own present, and helps in the effort to construct a more nuanced and well-informed portrait of Schubert for the future.

1 Representing Schubert: "A life devoted to art"

[Schubert] lived solely for art and for a small circle of friends
Obituary Notice, *Allgemeine Wiener Theaterzeitung*, 27 December 1828
(SMF 10)

Schubert had an image problem. During his lifetime, he was largely unknown beyond his native Vienna, where in any case the public was familiar with only a select portion of his vast output. After Schubert's death, scarce, inaccurate, and often conflicting information about him meant biographers and commentators could create almost any representation they fancied, the all-too-familiar portrait whose authenticity deserves a hard look. This introductory chapter examines Schubert's malleable image by contemplating the larger meanings of three important nineteenth-century pictures. Pondering specific visual depictions, I believe, can help us better understand Schubert's baffling place in the popular imagination. The sketch, sepia drawing, and painting reproduced here raise crucial issues concerning Schubert's compositions, cultural milieu, and general reputation. Even if this preliminary investigation does not ultimately yield the "real" Schubert, at the very least it alerts us to some of the complicating factors in representing his life.[1]

But before looking at these visual portraits, I should say a few words about the verbal portraits of the composer that have so powerfully informed public views. The first significant biography of

Schubert appeared nearly forty years after his death, an inconceivable lapse of time for any other leading nineteenth-century composer. No doubt a major reason for this delay was the unusual course of Schubert's lived and posthumous career, particularly that so many of his supreme compositions were only discovered long after his death. When Schubert died in 1828 at age thirty-one, few people would have considered his life worthy of a substantial book. Only in the mid 1860s did Heinrich Kreissle von Hellborn, a Viennese lawyer who had never met Schubert but who loved his music passionately, finally realize the task others had started yet never finished. In his lengthy biography Kreissle suggests another reason for the lack of interest: "Schubert is, perhaps, a single instance of a great artist whose outer life had no affinity or connection with his art. His career was so simple and uneventful, so out of all proportion with works that he created like a heavensent genius."[2] In short, Schubert's music is magnificent; his life is dull.

The composer's own family and friends had already sounded this familiar theme. Josef von Spaun (1788–1865), who arguably wrote the most detailed, reliable, but also the most protective reminiscences of his close friend, reacted quite negatively when Kreissle's book appeared late in 1864. He took issue with some of the musical observations offered, and even more with the portrayal of Schubert the man: "The biography contains too little light and too much shadow regarding Schubert as a human being" (SMF 362). Yet neither Spaun nor any other friend left a thoroughly convincing and compelling verbal portrait of the person they knew so well. Moreover, Schubert's own words are discouragingly limited. Fewer than a hundred of his letters survive, many fairly inconsequential. Aside from some scattered diary entries of 1816 and 1824, several poems, and a few pages known as "Mein Traum" (My Dream), no diaries, criticism, essays, or memoirs by Schubert have come down to us.

If we do not possess Schubert's own words in nearly the abundance we do Mozart's, Schumann's, or Wagner's, there does exist a good amount of testimony from others. Ultimately the letters, diaries, and memoirs written by family and friends provide the core information for a narrative of Schubert's life and the delineation of his character; they have proved indispensable to his biographers. The so-called Schubert Circle established a pattern of supporting and promoting its friend while he was alive, and it further sought to perpetuate certain views of him after his death. Some writings date from Schubert's lifetime, others came as memorial tributes immediately following his death, but the vast majority appeared many years later, after dear friend Schwammerl (an affectionate nickname meaning "little mushroom") had become a recognized Great Composer.

In fact, the evidence on which recent biographical conjectures about Schubert's sexuality and darker nature are based has been available for more than fifty years; most was published by the great Schubert scholar Otto Erich Deutsch in two magisterial collections of "documents" and "memoirs" (the essential SDB and SMF cited throughout this book). Revisionist scholars have rarely marshalled new material but, rather, like Dupin in Edgar Allan Poe's "The Purloined Letter," looked afresh at documents long in full public view. If these reinterpretations make use of familiar sources, what is novel are the connections made, the subtle readings and methodologies employed, and the critical imagination that attempts to conceive of Schubert free from the sentimental clichés of the past. Archival discoveries in the last few decades have substantially broadened our understanding of Schubert's cultural milieu, especially of his friends' lives, but unfortunately significant letters, diaries, or writings by the composer himself have not been found. Schubert remains in the shadows, even as some try figuratively to bring him out of the closet and the pub and into the psychiatrist's consulting room.

Although many friends and acquaintances described Schubert's physical appearance (often somewhat contradictorily), portraits supply the most compelling images.[3] Wilhelm August Rieder, an acquaintance of Schubert's, produced a famous watercolor that served as the basis for innumerable later illustrations (see illustration

1   Sketch by Ferdinand Georg Waldmüller of Schubert and friends (1827).

13, page 133). Schubert's nickname "Schwammerl" becomes much more concrete after one sees the caricature of the diminutive composer walking behind the towering singer Johann Michael Vogl (see illustration 7, page 58). Schubert's closest friend Franz von Schober (1796–1882) is said to have sketched these figures, and just as music was part of the general skills of many in Schubert's circle, so also was drawing. Two of his intimates, Leopold Kupelwieser (1796–1862) and Moritz von Schwind (1804–71), however, were far more than dilettantes; they were distinguished artists who executed many portraits of the composer.

The three depictions examined here enable us to consider Schubert in his contemporary context, as well as to chart briefly the changing representation of him over the course of the century. The first is by the distinguished Biedermeier artist Ferdinand Georg Waldmüller, who otherwise is not known to have been connected to Schubert. He sketched the composer informally singing with friends in a drawing that can be dated to late 1827. This primary source is, in fact, the closest thing we have to a "photograph" of Schubert in active music-making with friends, not all of whom have been identified.[4] The date and unusual scoring of the vocal trio (two males and a female) strongly suggest that they are singing *Der Hochzeitsbraten* (The Wedding Roast), a charming concoction to a trivial Schober text that was sure to delight all who heard it. This is Schubert enjoying music with friends, spontaneously and merrily.

All three of our illustrations, as well as many others dating from his own time, portray Schubert in the company of others. On the other hand, as befits the quintessential solitary creative genius, there are no known contemporaneous depictions in which Beethoven is placed together with anyone else. This is emblematic of Beethoven's relative isolation, in contrast to Schubert's far more social existence. The situation is likewise reflected in their respective musical reputations. While Beethoven's fame came from mighty masterpieces, primarily instrumental, Schubert was best known for small works, primarily vocal and keyboard. All three pictures capture this intimate, social, and domestic side of the Schubert. And yet the project of Schubert's maturity was to accomplish and to account for more.[5] In this he directly confronted the magnificent musical tradition bound to his native Vienna, and, more specifically, to the dominating artistic presence of Beethoven.

At the end of the eighteenth century, Vienna, still at the center of the Holy Roman Empire, was in the midst of a musical golden age. The roughly seventy years (1760s-1828) that span Haydn's maturity and Mozart's entire career, and that conclude with the deaths of Beethoven and Schubert, saw not only the glories of the Classical style and the birth of musical Romanticism, but also striking changes in musical culture, such as the beginnings of modern concert life and the forging of a new status for musicians working as independent creative artists. Much of the music and musical life that we know and value today emerged during this remarkable period. Beethoven is the pivotal figure, the bridge between Classic past and Romantic future. Blessed by Mozart (who supposedly predicted that he would go far) and for a time fitfully taught by Haydn, Beethoven was the imposing model for many composers who followed him. Moreover, his ultimate authority came as much from the aesthetic creed he embodied as from the music he wrote. One can scarcely imagine the solitary Beethoven wearing a powdered wig or bowing to anyone, as Haydn and Mozart had. Schubert, too, let his hair grow free.

Schubert studied and cherished this outstanding musical heritage, although he lived a quite dissimilar existence from that of his predecessors. A truly freelance composer, without title or station, Schubert died just twenty months after Beethoven – a generation younger, yet his contemporary. While Rossini's operas delighted Viennese audiences beginning in 1816, and Paganini's wizardry dazzled them in 1828, Beethoven towered artistically above them all, and the musical world knew it. Schubert genuinely admired Rossini ("You cannot deny him extraordinary genius") and was overwhelmed after hearing Paganini play ("Tonight I heard an angel sing"), but Beethoven consumed his thoughts. If Schubert had a "Beethoven complex," it was something he shared with most later nineteenth-century composers.

Such was the context in which Schubert gradually established an unrepresentative kind of fame during the 1820s. The musical genres for which he was most familiar were quite different from those which eventually won his immortality or which audiences usually encounter today in concerts or on recordings. Among the small-scale genres occasioning such intimate music-making as Waldmüller sketched, Lieder won pride of place, although Schubert's popularity and success also came from dances, partsongs (usually for two tenors and two basses), and keyboard music (especially four-hand compositions). Whereas Mozart, Beethoven, and others first made their names as virtuoso pianists, Schubert, a performer of far more limited talent, earned more modest recognition through the popular types of compositions. This constituted his sole musical accomplishment in the eyes of many during the early part of the century.

But like his imposing predecessors, Schubert, too, had higher aspirations and during the 1820s he increasingly composed ambitious dramatic, religious, keyboard, chamber, and orchestral works intended for a wide public. His contemporaries knew only a few of these "higher" compositions; hence the discrepancy between Schubert's lived and posthumous fame, as well as between the image of him as a song and dance composer and as a serious master. The larger musical implications of Waldmüller's sketch for Schubert's biography are clear: we must know what music, in what genres, we are talking about at various stages of his career.

Late in life, nearly forty years after Schubert's death, Moritz von Schwind crafted his famous "Schubertiade at Josef von Spaun's," which features a grand party of familiar Schubertians. Although Schubert figured prominently in many of Schwind's drawings and paintings, this particular project held special importance for the artist, who by the 1860s was one of the most notable in central Europe. After completing a preliminary sketch, Schwind wrote to the poet Eduard Mörike: "I have begun to work at something which I feel I owe

2 Sepia drawing by Moritz von Schwind of a Schubertiade at Josef von Spaun's (1865).

the intellectual part of Germany – my admirable friend Schubert at the piano, surrounded by his circle of listeners. I know all the people by heart."[6]

If Waldmüller's sketch prompts us to consider the nature of music-making among Schubert's friends, Schwind's elegant and more substantial representation raises the question of who exactly all these people were. Although composers inevitably have friends, collaborators, and champions, Schubert's entire existence seems unusually involved with a group of friends, mainly young men often quite distinguished in their own right, with whom he lived, worked, traveled, and socialized. Schubert's background differed considerably from most of them. Born into a modest, although not poor, family, Schubert was blessed with a phenomenal musical talent. As a scholarship student at an excellent boarding school, Schubert came into contact with fellow students, as well as with their extended network of families and friends, most of whom were of higher social status. (The "von" in many names testifies to their privileged positions.) Friends gave the young Schubert manuscript paper when he had none, introduced him to a vast spectrum of the arts, and actively promoted his music with publishers and performers. A few provided housing, sometimes for years at a time, and determined the course of his daily life in myriad ways.

Later, these individuals told Schubert's story to posterity. Whereas prominent public figures usually begin at some point to mold their own reception (Wagner is a notorious example), Schubert did not live long enough to do so. Thus it was up to those who remained behind to establish his image, albeit with varying degrees of knowledge, insight, and candor. While for many composers a spouse, family member, or friend so dominates their emotional life that a single relationship becomes a central biographical issue (think of Robert and Clara Schumann), Schubert's ties were much looser and more varied. As far as we can tell, Schubert's family, except for his older brother Ferdinand, played a relatively minor role after his teenage years, although he went back to live with them on various occasions and would visit when he lived elsewhere. Schubert never married, nor apparently was there any sustained and mutual love affair with a woman. Instead, except for some troubled and troubling periods, the core group of male friends was the essential and ever present reality of his daily existence year after year.

Schwind completed the final sepia version of his picture in 1868 (an oil painting of the same design was left unfinished), and even today nearly every individual in it can be identified. He grouped participants according to their creative field: the artists Rieder, Schwind, and Kupelwieser stand together behind the seated ladies; literary friends – Franz Grillparzer, Johann Senn, Johann Baptist Mayrhofer, Ignaz Castelli, Eduard von Bauernfeld – are at the extreme right. The host of pre-eminent Schubertiades, Josef von Spaun, sits on the composer's left. Spaun long played the role of best friend, loyal and devoted, although not necessarily the most intimate or influential. The two first met in 1808 at the school dormitory where they lived, and Spaun quickly took Schubert, nine years his junior, under his wing. It was Spaun, a law student at the time, who supplied the music paper and enabled Schubert during vacations to see operas such as Gluck's *Iphigenia in Tauris* and Josef Weigl's *Das Waisenhaus* and *Die Schweizerfamilie*, thereby exposing Schubert not only to the works themselves, but also to performers such as Vogl and the famous soprano Anna Milder. Spaun also introduced Schubert to many of his friends from his native Linz. Later Spaun fondly remembered how "all became friends and brothers together. It was a beautiful, unforgettable time" (SMF 130).

Schubert accompanies Vogl, sitting on his right. Twenty-nine years the composer's senior and perhaps more mentor than close confidant, Vogl, Spaun felt, "might be regarded as Schubert's second father: he not only took care of him materially, but in truth furthered him also spiritually and artistically" (SMF 14). A *divo* who translated classical Greek texts to pass the time, Vogl could be a prickly personality with stringent moral standards. According to one acquaintance, Adam Haller, "Schubert alone, or rather his genius, possessed the magic to tame this rough nature" (SMF 56). Vogl's professional efforts played a vital role in launching Schubert's career. He also introduced him to important patrons and cultural luminaries, and provided advice and financial assistance, especially on the long journeys Schubert and he took together during certain summers. The eminent singer lent some stability to Schubert's life, in sharp contrast to the youthful exploits of Schober and Company, which one of Vogl's biographers deemed "the most dissolute circles of university students, artists, poets, and theater people" (SMF 162). By the time Schwind depicts, Vogl was retired from the operatic stage and rarely performed in public. Schubert's songs preoccupied his last twenty years, and he sang them frequently at private gatherings until his death, in 1840, at age seventy-two.

Two other figures rendered under Schwind's keen eye deserve special mention. A portrait of Countess Caroline von Esterházy, a student of Schubert's for whom he evidently possessed an idealized love, serves as muse above the guests, a fact worth noting for later discussions. Another significant touch – and a compelling commentary – is Schwind's visual reproach of Schober, seated in the second row on the far right and the sole participant not entranced by Schubert's music; he is rather more interested in flirting with the lovely Justina von Bruchmann sitting next to him.

Schober held particular importance for Schubert. Today, we might characterize him as charismatic. Clearly he cast a spell, not only over Schubert, who lived with him and his mother for extended periods. (They even merged their names into one: Schobert.) Born in Sweden a year before his friend, Schober came from a wealthy family whose fortunes kept falling under the weight of his mismanagement and extravagant living. Talented in several of the arts and apparently passionate about them all, Schober lacked the discipline and formidable talent of other friends – the literary skills of Senn, Mayrhofer, and Bauernfeld, the artistic gifts of Kupelwieser and Schwind – and he could scarcely hope to compete with the special genius of his musical companion. Nearly everyone adulated Schober, many sincerely. Schubert once wrote to him in a letter, "Your understanding of art is the purest and truest imaginable" (SDB 98).

Schober facilitated a vibrant intellectual, cultural, and artistic atmosphere for Schubert and exerted a profound influence on his art by suggesting what the composer read and set to music, and even by providing his own words for a dozen songs and an opera (*Alfonso und Estrella*). Many years after first introducing them, Spaun gave a generous assessment of Schober's importance for Schubert, emphasizing

> the great services rendered by the extremely talented Schober with his burning enthusiasm for art. Schober, with his mother's permission, repeatedly received Schubert into his home and gave him many proofs of his friendship and his care. In particular, Schober is deserving of the greatest credit in regard to Schubert for having brought about the latter's association with Vogl, which was achieved only after great difficulties. The society of a young man so enthusiastic about art and of such refined culture as Schober, himself a successful poet, could clearly have only the most stimulating and favorable effect on Schubert. Schober's friends also became Schubert's friends, and I am convinced that living among this circle of people was far more advantageous to Schubert than if he had lived among a circle of musicians and professional colleagues, though he did not neglect these either. (SMF 363–64)

At once at the center of a remarkable group of young men, Schober was ultimately distinguished by mediocrity, laziness, and, in the eyes of some contemporaries, as we shall see, loose living. When the writer Eduard von Bauernfeld (1802–90) finally met Schober in 1825, after having heard about him for years, they "at once began an agreeable relationship" and even lived together briefly. Bauernfeld's first reaction was that even though many "worship him like a god, I find him pretty human, but interesting." His opinion had not much changed eight months later, when he wrote in his diary, "Schober surpasses us all in mind, and even more so in speech! Yet there is much about him that is artificial, and his best powers threaten to be suffocated by idleness" (SDB 428, 516). Bauernfeld left a trenchant commentary in a

New Year's sketch from 1826 in which Schober is cast as the lazy and corrupting Pantaloon (SDB 486–502). Although Schwind also long worshiped Schober, the place he assigned him in the Schubertiade representation reveals his eventual disenchantment.

The aura of Schwind's visual Schubertiade is unabashedly nostalgic and offers up a sanitized Vienna seemingly without political repression, daily hardships, or emotional cares. Remembering the brief time Schubert and he lived door-to-door, Schwind told the composer Ferdinand Hiller: "There could be no happier existence. Each morning he composed something beautiful and each evening he found the most enthusiastic admirers. We gathered in his room – he played and sang to us – we were enthusiastic and afterwards we went to the tavern. We hadn't a penny but were blissfully happy" (SMF 283). Such nostalgia, we shall see, permeates not only this and other images, but also many of the writings of Schubert's circle, and even some of the music Schubert composed and others arranged.

Near the end of Schubert's life, Bauernfeld wrote in his diary of a "gap in the friends' circle ... What is to become of us all? Shall we stick together?" (SDB 661). In fact, after Schubert's death friends did drift apart even more, not so much because Schubert had been the glue that had held them together, as because the late 1820s marked a time during which adult life circumstances – marriage, jobs, artistic fame – meant that many went their own way. Therefore much of the nostalgia that colors images of Schubert's life comes from the fact that when friends discussed or pictured Schubert, they were looking back on their own lost youth as well.

As Schwind's image shows, Schubert provided the musical focus for many social gatherings. The image is deceiving, however, in a number of respects. Although friends often referred to themselves as a "circle," sometimes even the "Schubert Circle," such a label implies a single group with a fixed constituency, and further suggests that Schubert was the origin and center – neither of which is true. In fact, Schubert and his friends often allude to a "circle" (*Kreis*), "society" (*Gesellschaft*), or "club" (*Verein*) in describing a range of both formal and informal associations that comprise a variety of participants and activities. The Gesellschaft der Musikfreunde, Vienna's musical society, boasted a large and distinguished membership of passionate amateurs and professionals, and Schubert worked his way up to prominence in that organization. The secret societies with which his name was linked included individuals he knew from school or from elsewhere in Viennese cultural life. The informal "reading society" in which Schubert participated held regularly scheduled meetings where serious conversation was highly valued, if not always achieved. The "pub crawlers" (as they called themselves) with whom Schubert, after a long day composing, would spend many hours, many nights a week, were a varied and informal group of old friends and new acquaintances. Not only was there no unchanging circle of friends, but the particular people Schwind includes in his Schubertiade were never all in one room together, and a few never even met Schubert or one another.

Whereas Schwind represented events he knew from personal experience, however nostalgically, our third image is pure fiction, created by an artist who had no connection with Schubert. Julius Schmid was commissioned to paint his bourgeois Schubertiade to commemorate the 1897 centennial of the composer's birth. He shows Schubert and his elegant audience in a lush setting that would not be out of place on a Hollywood movie stage. The immediacy of Waldmüller's sketch, and the brio of Schwind's intensely personal drawing and the loving accuracy of its group portrait, have here devolved into a falsely dramatized image of the genius at the keyboard taking requests from his audience. Schmid's painting epitomizes the trivialization of Schubert found in countless medleys, novels, and operettas at the opening of the twentieth century, most notoriously Heinrich Berté's tremendously successful operetta *Das Dreimäderlhaus* (1916), based on Rudolph Hans Bartsch's best-selling Schubert novel *Schwammerl* (1912). Film versions of Berté's operetta, especially the adaption starring Richard Tauber, as well as English versions called *Lilac Time* and

3 Oil painting by Julius Schmid of a Schubertiade (1897).

Blossom Time, were also hugely popular. The influence of such seductively ingratiating kitsch is difficult to counter and reverse. The meek Schubert who loves but never wins the girl, who writes beautiful music only to be neglected by all but his faithful friends, who was so poor and died so young – this sentimental view reached its height at the *fin de siècle*, especially in Vienna. Many of these themes linger to this day.

All three of our Schubert representations may make us wonder exactly what compositions are being played (and heard) within them. As mentioned, the date of the Waldmüller sketch, and the performers depicted, indicate a specific vocal trio from 1827. We might like to think, as Schubert's biographer Maurice J. E. Brown suggested, that Schwind presents Vogl and Schubert playing the wondrous song *An die Musik*, Schubert's ode to his beloved art that sets Schober's sentimental words. And in the Schmid painting, one can imagine a large variety of pieces intended to delight listeners. Music is at the inaudible center of all three depictions, and points to the fact that it is the music that ultimately makes us care about Schubert's life.

In truth, Schubert's compositions themselves assume unusual biographical importance and not just because they may, as is often the case, reflect specific events in the composer's life. We wonder what sort of man would conceive such pieces: beautiful, sad, convivial, dark – a long list of apparently contradictory qualities – and begin to construct an image of Schubert based on personal responses. Many compositions suggest a carefree soul who must have loved to sing and make music with and for friends. Other pieces seem almost private mediations written for no intended audience. (Schubert persistently composed ambitious works without any prospect of performance or publication.) There are hints of deep religious feeling in some compositions; at the same time Schubert's Masses consistently undercut institutional dogma. He was obsessed with death throughout his career, and typically Viennese darker forces often lurk beneath the gaiety. The frequent wistfulness, the laughing through tears (or crying with laughter), conspire to seduce us into believing we know something of the man who expresses himself in such ways.

Ultimately, however, the images we construct are projections of our own feelings, desires, and interests; they do not really tell us much about Schubert the man. So we inevitably connect Schubert's music with what we know – or think we know – about his life in hazy outline: he loved his friends, his health was poor (as were his finances), he wrote quickly and intuitively, he died young. The tendency to relate Schubert's music to his biography is epitomized by the popular "Unfinished" Symphony, which seems a perfect metaphor for an "unfinished" life. (In point of fact, this extraordinary work was not silenced by death; Schubert had put it aside years earlier.) The urge to make such musical and biographical connections was encouraged by Schubert's friends. A year after Schubert died, Bauernfeld wrote in a memorial tribute that "so far as it is possible to draw conclusions as to a man's character and mind from his artistic products, those will not go astray who judge Schubert from his songs to have been a man full of affection and goodness of heart" (SMF 31).

A hundred years after Schmid's lavish illustration, no single visual image symbolizes the postmodern Schubert; instead, we have a new conceptual portrait of a darker, neurotic composer. An impressive oil painting, recently identified as depicting the young Schubert (some dispute this claim), graces the covers of books, scores, CDs, and concert programs.[7] Many people react, "Well, that certainly doesn't look like Schubert." This is rather like the response to the new image of Schubert as gay, drunk, and depressed, "Well, that certainly doesn't seem like Schubert." Ultimately, Schubert may get lost in images that tend to reflect the time of the observer, and which serve diverse purposes and interests, more than that capture the historical realities of Schubert's perhaps not-so-dull life.

2 Young Schubert: "The master in the boy"

The small public which surrounded the composer during the first years of his musical activity, consisting only of his family, some of his classmates and a few friends who already recognized the master in the boy, gradually increased.

Josef von Spaun, 1829 (SMF 20)

Vienna's golden musical age drew its glory from transplanted genius. Gluck, Haydn, Mozart, and Beethoven, not to mention such lesser lights as Salieri, Gyrowetz, and Hummel, all gravitated to this celebrated musical city, capital of the Austrian Empire, which was and is so attractive to immigrants generally. Alone among the great composers of this era, Franz Schubert was born there, on 31 January 1797, where his parents had settled two decades earlier.

Of Schubert's first years we have scant knowledge, although some revealing information can be gleaned from parish records and other documents. A marriage register in Lichtental, the modest suburb not far outside the city walls, near where Schubert would be born twelve years later, records on 17 January 1785 that "Franz Schuberth [sic], a school instructor, native of Neudorf in Moravia, farmer's son, Lichtental No. 152, Catholic, 25 years old, single" married "Elisabeth Vitzin [Vietz], native of Zuckmantel in Imperial Silesia, master locksmith's daughter, Lichtental No. 152, Catholic, 28 years old, single." One of their two witnesses was the bridegroom's brother, Karl

Schubert, who seven years later married Elisabeth's younger sister Magdalene. A birth-register entry less than two months later casts some further light on this union: the birth of a son, Ignaz Franz. We also learn that Schubert's father was not twenty-five at the time of his marriage, but twenty-two, nearly seven years younger than his pregnant bride. During the next three decades, the hard-working Franz Theodor Florian Schubert built a distinguished career as an educator, while Elisabeth was consumed with annual pregnancies and with needy young children who were frequently ill. Nine of their fourteen children died in infancy:

Ignaz Franz	8 March 1785–30 November 1844
Elisabeth	1 March 1786–12 August 1788
Karl	23 April 1787–6 February 1788
Franziska Magdalena	6 June 1788–13 August 1788
Franziska Magdalena	5 July 1789–1 January 1792
Franz Karl	10 August 1790–10 September 1790
Anna Karolina	11 July 1791–29 July 1791
Petrus	29 June 1792–14 January 1793
Josef	16 September 1793–18 October 1798
Ferdinand Lukas	18 October 1794–26 February 1859
Franz Karl	5 November 1795–20 March 1855
Franz Peter Schubert	31 January 1797–19 November 1828
Aloisia Magdalena	17 December 1799–18 December 1799
Maria Theresia	17 September 1801–7 August 1878

The family first lived in a house named Zum roten Krebsen (The Red Crayfish), in a suburb of Vienna called the Himmelpfortgrund (Heaven's Gate). Schubert's birth took place in an alcove located off the one room his family occupied above the ground floor. Through diligent work and long hours, Schubert's father was able, in late 1801, to purchase a building not far away, Zum schwarzen Rössel (The Black Horse), which not only served as the family living quarters, but also housed the school he ran. This school, which Schubert and his brothers attended, grew rapidly and had some 300 students by 1804.[1]

4 Pen and ink drawing by Erwin Pendl of Schubert's Birth House in the Himmelpfortgrund (1897).

The Schubert sons were expected eventually to join the family business. The first-born, Ignaz, a hunchback, worked as an assistant and took control upon his father's death in 1830. Schubert's letters show a special affinity with Ignaz as a fellow free-thinker, often opposed to their stern, devout, patriotic, and dogmatic father. Ferdinand appears to have been the closest brother, judging from their correspondence and from his attentive care of Schubert during the composer's last ten weeks of life. In the mid-1820s, during an extremely difficult period, Schubert wrote Ferdinand a remarkable letter that talked of their shared strong emotions: "You, and only you, are my truest friend, bound to my soul with every fiber!" (SDB 363). Ferdinand, though the second-eldest son, was the leader of the younger generation and a beneficiary of the sale of family property, while Ignaz was not. Himself a fine musician (his principal instruments were organ and violin) and competent composer, Ferdinand began teaching at his father's school in 1810 and, after holding various other positions, taught at the

k. k. Normalhauptschule (Imperial and Royal Training College) in the Annagasse, of which he eventually became director. Schubert referred to Karl, a fine painter and just fifteen months his senior, as his "double brother" in life and in art. Karl remains a shadowy figure. No letters survive between them, although in 1828 Schubert contacted various influential friends in Graz to request that they support Karl's bid for a position there teaching drawing.

As there were few professional possibilities available to women, little is known about Schubert's sister Maria Theresia, called Resi, except for some information concerning her childbearing. In 1824, Ferdinand apprised Schubert that,

> Brother Karl is blessed with a little Ferdinand, to whom I stood godfather, and who is still alive; but Resi, who gave birth to a strong and healthy girl, was not granted that happiness for long, for the infant lived only twelve or fourteen days. Grief at the death of her first-born nearly turned to raving madness and confined her to the sick-bed for several weeks. Fortunately she has now got past the danger of serious trouble and seems to be resigned to her fate. (SDB 378)

The childhood of a composer is usually investigated only retrospectively, after fame is secure and the subject deemed worthy of attention. Posthumous accounts written by Schubert's family and friends many years later give testimony, no doubt occasionally exaggerated and inaccurate, about the youthful origins and evidence of his genius. Although he did not come from a family of professional musicians, as had Bach, Mozart, and Beethoven, Schubert's first musical experiences were likewise domestic and familial. His father later recalled that when Schubert was eight he "taught him the necessary rudiments of violin playing and trained him to the point of being able to play easy duets quite well." Ignaz was astonished when, after just a few months of teaching his brother the piano, Schubert "announced to me that he no longer needed my further instruction and he now wanted to continue on his own" (SMF 212).

Schubert served as violist in the family quartet. Ferdinand led from the violins' first stand, Ignaz took the second, and their father played cello (not always so well, we are told). Although the young Schubert quickly surpassed the abilities of his father and brothers, he continued to play with them, an activity that had considerable impact on his compositional development. During the 1810s, Schubert would write about half of his twenty or so string quartets for this family ensemble (a few of them are unfinished or lost).

Franz Theodor soon realized that his precocious son required professional instruction and therefore turned to Michael Holzer (1772–1826), choirmaster and organist at the local parish church in Lichtental. Holzer's famous remark – "If I wanted to teach him something new, he already knew it" – may never have been uttered, but it is forever recounted as proof of Schubert's god-given talents. In 1858, Josef von Spaun related a similar comment from Schubert's school days: after just two lessons, Wenzel Ruzicka supposedly remarked, "I can teach him nothing, he has learnt it from God himself" (SMF 34, 128; cf. 145, 212, 362). Such amazed benedictions serve to legitimate Schubert's natural genius at the same time as they tend to obscure the scope of his actual training and reliance on practical models. Perhaps more important than Holzer's guidance in singing, organ, and theory was the regular exposure Schubert gained at the church to a wide variety of great music, and the new opportunities he enjoyed of participating in a much higher level of performance than he experienced at home. This church's archives still hold late eighteenth- and nineteenth-century copies of sacred and chamber music by Mozart, Joseph and Michael Haydn, and minor masters, that must have been revelatory to Schubert's budding genius.

Domestic music-making, involvement at the Lichtental Church, and studies with Holzer, as well as a naturally fine singing voice, all combined to make Schubert an especially attractive candidate for a coveted musical scholarship that might lead to further opportunities. As early as age seven, on 28 September 1804, Schubert underwent examination by Antonio Salieri, Imperial Court Kapellmeister and the dominant musical authority of the day, and was among nine of nineteen boys deemed "most capable to learn the chant for the service of music in the Court Chapel."[2] In August 1808, when Schubert was eleven, the *Wiener Zeitung* announced a competition to fill three boy soprano positions in the Imperial Court Chapel. Schubert was one of the chosen, and with this honor came a free general education at the Akademisches Gymnasium (Academic Grammar Gymnasium). Schubert's preparation at his father's "German" school was good enough for him to handle the rigors of a much more prestigious "Latin" gymnasium. Report cards indicate that Schubert was a good student, with recurring special commendations of his "excellent" musical talent. The education Schubert received was conservative and heavily weighted toward the classics.[3]

The ten young choristers of the Court Chapel and other gymnasium students, as well as older university students and instructors, were housed at the k. k. Stadtkonvikt (The Imperial and Royal City Seminary). It was while living there, beginning in the fall of 1808, that Schubert met many of the friends who would play such a significant role in his life. Josef von Spaun, one of the first and most important of them, introduced Schubert to many of his own friends from Linz and the nearby Kremsmünster Seminary. Away from home for the first time, Schubert may have initially felt lonely and isolated; various Seminary friends later reported that he generally kept to himself. Spaun states that Schubert once told him, "You are my favorite in the whole Seminary, I have no other friend here," and that he "did not seem to find the institution congenial, for the little boy was always serious and not very amiable" (SMF 127, 125). Schubert was particularly sorry when, in September 1809, Spaun returned to Linz for eighteen months.

Music was surely Schubert's salvation during this time, as the Seminary promoted an extremely active musical life. The Lichtental Church and the Court Chapel Choir exposed Schubert to masterpieces of sacred music, he was constantly discovering chamber music with family and friends, and now activities at the Seminary opened up a new world of orchestral music through an ensemble that played most nights after dinner. Schubert's classmate Anton Holzapfel recalled that

> year in and year out, at our daily performances all the symphonies of Josef Haydn and Mozart, the first two symphonies of Beethoven, as well as all the Overtures we could tackle at that time . . . were regularly performed, and we also played through the greater part of the classical quartets of Haydn and Mozart; everything, of course, extremely roughly and inaccurately and on bad instruments. (SMF 58)

Spaun, who admits to being one of the poorer musicians, thought the Seminary's director was making fun of him when he placed him in charge of the orchestra, but his organizational and leadership skills meant that he proved a good choice. Schubert initially played from the same second-violin stand as Spaun and slowly became more important to the ensemble, even conducting as principal violin when Ruzicka was away. This amateur but dedicated orchestra thus nightly exposed Schubert to the great music of the recent past, and within just a few years was the first ensemble to read through Schubert's own early overtures and symphonies.

Ferdinand Schubert recollected that his brother's earliest keyboard composition was a long fantasy for piano duet; the thirteen-year-old composer precisely dated this work: "begun on 8 April and completed 1 May 1810." Otto Erich Deutsch designated the piece as D1 in his authoritative catalogue of Schubert's complete works.[4] Schubert had already written smaller pieces – Spaun called the fantasy his "first larger work" (SMF 19); in any case, all these initial compositions were apprentice exercises, some of which were performed privately by friends and family. That Schubert composed at all went unmentioned for many years in any official document; public performances and publications were likewise nearly a decade off.

Schubert's musical horizons broadened each year that he spent at the Seminary. He played chamber music, sang in small vocal ensembles, and encountered a vast array of music by established composers, some of which he would copy out himself. Early defining influences were not limited to the great classical masters, but also included relatively minor figures. The religious music and male partsongs of Michael Haydn, younger brother of Joseph, are one case. Even more important were the songs of Johann Rudolf Zumsteeg, considered among the best Lied composers at the turn of the century. For Schubert, experimenting on his own, imitation proved an invaluable learning experience. Spaun reports coming across Schubert one day at the Seminary: "He had several of Zumsteeg's songs in front of him and told me that these songs moved him profoundly . . . He said he could revel in these songs for days on end. And to this youthful predilection of his we probably owe the direction Schubert took, and yet how little of an imitator he was and how independent the path he followed." In Spaun's words, Schubert "wanted to modernize Zumsteeg's song form" (SMF 127). *Hagars Klage* is Schubert's earliest complete song to survive. Written at the Seminary and dated 30 March 1811, the sixteen-minute piece draws on a story from the Bible's book of Genesis. Others of Schubert's earliest Lieder were concretely modeled on Zumsteeg, not simply imitating his style, but going so far as to borrow extended structures. Schubert would set the same poems, adapt the formal mold, and sometimes use the same keys and meters to build long, discursive songs. (A handful of Schubert's early songs are more than ten minutes long; *Der Taucher* lasts some twenty-four minutes.) Spaun was undoubtedly correct: Schubert's indirect, though inspiring, encounter with a composer now relegated to a footnote in music history held great importance for the development of the German Lied.

Another significant early influence was far more personal. Schubert had first come into contact with Salieri, Vienna's famous Kapellmeister who most famously did not murder Mozart, at age seven when he sang the preliminary audition for the Court Chapel Choir. Schubert was later granted special permission to take private lessons with Salieri, which meant leaving school several times each week. A marginal note in Schubert's hand to an elementary exercise reads "counterpoint begun, 18 June 1812, first species" (SDB 24). Spaun (corroborated by other evidence) states that "even after his young protégé had left the Imperial Court Chapel, its musical director, Salieri, showed a special partiality for him and for several years gave him almost daily instruction in composition, which took root in good soil." At Salieri's, Schubert first met his close friend Anselm Hüttenbrenner, who later remembered that "from time to time Salieri treated his pupils, Schubert among them, to ice cream, which was obtainable from a lemonade kiosk in the Graben" (SMF 19, 68).

For some years, I think, Salieri was Schubert's idealized artistic father figure, a position that Beethoven ultimately came to fill. Evidence of Schubert's genuine devotion to his illustrious teacher – Schubert enjoyed a certain fame by association – is found in works dedicated to him and in a diary entry written in 1816 after he had attended a celebration of the fiftieth anniversary of the Italian composer's arrival in Vienna: "It must be beautiful and refreshing for an artist to see all his pupils gathered about him, each one striving to give his best for his jubilee, and to hear in all these compositions the expression of pure nature" (SDB 64). Salieri apparently hoped to make an opera composer out of Schubert. Their studies together concentrated on counterpoint and Italian vocal music, as is evident in some of Salieri's annotations that survive. Spaun relates that the two eventually reached an impasse: "When Salieri repeatedly took Schubert seriously to task for occupying himself with poems in the barbarous German language and requested him not to compose anything more at all in German, but rather to set insignificant Italian poems, Schubert lost patience" (SMF 130; cf. 19). Nevertheless, Schubert proudly, and perhaps even shrewdly, identified himself as Salieri's student. He mentioned their association when applying for jobs and announced it prominently on the title pages of some of his most ambitious young compositions. Early reviews of Schubert often referred to him as a "pupil of our much-venerated Salieri." The cover of the three-act Singspiel *Des Teufels Lustschloss* (1813–14) cites the composer as the "pupil of Herr Salieri, First Imperial and Royal Court Kapellmeister in Vienna." Schubert wrote two complete versions of the work under his teacher's watchful eye.

Once the trickle of composing began, it quickly became a torrent. Deutsch's catalogue lists some 1,000 works, starting with the four-hand keyboard fantasy and concluding with what was likely Schubert's last completed work, *Die Taubenpost* (D965A), from October 1828.[5] Some three quarters of this oeuvre, more than 700 pieces, was written during Schubert's first decade of activity, before 1821, when he began achieving public recognition with publications and prominent public performances. His creative energies, more-over, found expression in almost every important musical genre. While still living at the Seminary, Schubert wrote songs, dances, chamber music, religious works, and piano works, as well as an unfinished opera, *Der Spiegelritter*, and his First Symphony (D82).

Throughout his life, Schubert's music provided a tangible chronicle of growth and change. The young Robert Schumann expressed this beautifully: "What a diary is to others, in which their momentary emotions and so forth are recorded, so to Schubert was music paper, to which he entrusted all his moods. His thoroughly musical soul wrote notes where others used words."[6] Particularly in his early years, Schubert precisely dated nearly every composition and there-fore they do become something of a diary of his growth, which proves especially valuable given that so few of his letters or other writings survive.

Even an event as momentous as his mother's death – at age fifty-five on Corpus Christi Day, 28 May 1812 – goes unremarked. We can only guess the reaction to this trauma, although much speculation about the aftermath of her death has been fueled by a few pages Schubert wrote ten years later. This famous document – "Mein Traum" – may record a dream (the title, however, is written in Ferdinand's hand at the end of the last page) or else may be a fictional story of some kind. The "dream" is narrated by a musician and begins:

I was the brother of many brothers and sisters. Our father and mother were good people. I was deeply and lovingly devoted to them all. Once my father took us to a feast. There my brothers became very merry. I, however, was sad. Then my father approached me and bade me enjoy the delicious dishes. But I could not, whereupon my father, becoming angry, banished me from his sight. I turned my footsteps and, my heart full of infinite love for those who disdained it, I wandered into far-off regions. For long years I felt torn between the greatest grief and the greatest love. And so the news of my mother's death reached me. I hastened to see her, and my father, mellowed with sorrow, did not hinder my entrance. Then I saw her corpse. Tears flowed from my eyes.

After another falling out, the musician set out once more: "For many and many a year I sang songs. Whenever I attempted to sing of love, it turned to pain. And again, when I tried to sing of pain, it turned to love. Thus were love and pain divided in me." A final reunion between father and son took place at the grave of a gentle maiden: "I felt as though eternal bliss were gathered together into a single moment. My father too I saw, reconciled and loving. He took me in his arms and wept. But not as much as I" (SDB 226–28).

The story contains certain parallels with events in Schubert's life, but other parts of it do not correlate with any known facts. In the absence of further information about his mother's death and its effects on Schubert and the rest of the family, or about the relationship between father and son, there has been a strong temptation to view "Mein Traum" as autobiographical. Psychoanalytic studies have offered a wide range of interpretations, exploring the text's symbolism and suggesting that it may reveal Schubert's homosexuality or that Schubert's father may have abused him. Arnold Schering believed the narrative was the "secret program" of the "Unfinished" Symphony, written not long after. Maurice J. E. Brown proposed that it might have been a "word game" played among the Schubertians, and Ilija Dürhammer has noted that it is similar in many respects to *Die Lehrlinge zu Saïs*, a short story by Novalis, and may have been a literary exercise of some sort. Whether recording an actual dream or a living fantasy, the suggestive writing may give a rare glimpse into Schubert's psychological make-up and relationship to his family.[7]

Barely eleven months after his mother's death, Schubert's father, then age forty-nine, remarried. His bride was the thirty-year-old Anna Kleyenböck, who during the next thirteen years bore him five children, one of whom died. Schubert's relations with his young stepmother, as well as with his four younger siblings, appear to have been affectionate. In letters he addressed her as "mother," and on occasion she is said to have given him money (SMF 256; cf. 361).

Schubert's first surviving letter was written to one of his brothers (we are not sure which) at the beginning of his fifth and final year at the Seminary, in the fall after his mother's death. It is a charming appeal for some extra cash to make life a bit easier. Schubert states that he has "long been thinking about [his] situation and found that, although it is satisfactory on the whole, it is not beyond some improvement here and there." He sounds the eternal complaint of boarding school captives – the food is bad – and says the small allowance father provides disappears immediately "to the devil." If his brother could therefore give him a bit more each month, money which would never be missed at home, life would improve greatly for the fifteen-year-old. To bolster his request, he misattributes two scriptural passages, perhaps intentionally, and signs off "Your loving, poor, hopeful and again poor brother Franz" (SDB 28).

A *Wiener Zeitung* announcement of a new competition for two boy sopranos in the summer of 1812 signals the end of Schubert's tenure in the Court Chapel Choir. (More humorously, Schubert's change of voice is commemorated in the alto part for Peter Winter's Mass in C, in which he scribbled, "Schubert, Franz, crowed for the last time, 26 July 1812".) Although his service in the Choir was now over, Schubert was eligible for fellowships that would have allowed him to continue his studies. He had completed the first of a two-year humanities sequence, which would be followed by two more upper-level years before university. By this stage in his academic career, Schubert's extraordinary musical talents were apparent to everyone, but his progress in other areas had fallen off – how could they not have, given so much composing? – and in the case of mathematics proved unsatisfactory. Rectifying that deficiency would have been necessary were Schubert to have accepted one of the endowed fellowships for which he was nominated.

Ferdinand Schubert states that his brother "left the Seminary owing to his extraordinary attachment to music," which Spaun confirms more poetically: Schubert "decided, with this father's consent, to leave the Seminary and to give up his studies as well, in order to be able to devote his life to art undisturbed" (SMF 36, 19; cf. 13, 24, 26). Schubert was strengthened in his resolve during a conversation with Spaun and the young poet Theodor Körner after a revelatory performance of Gluck's *Iphigenia in Tauris* at the Kärntnertor-Theater in January 1813. Spaun remembered how the already famous poet, who would soon die, "encouraged Schubert to live for art," saying that this was the path to happiness (SMF 129).

Even had Schubert wished only to compose, this activity would not have supported him, and thus there must have been considerable pressure from home to find a secure career. Spaun and others agree that Schubert's father "was dead set against [Schubert's] devoting himself to music" (SMF 127), and that he wanted him to become a teacher like himself, his uncle, and his older brothers. One senses a certain familial pride in his father's unsuccessful petition for a position for himself in 1815, when he states that "his four sons are all already in the service of the elementary school organization" (SDB 48). At age sixteen, after five years at the Seminary in the inner city, Schubert moved back to his family home and began in November 1813 to attend classes at the teacher-training school of the k. k. Normalhauptschule in the Annagasse. Six times a week, Schubert would walk from the Himmelpfortgrund to the inner city with his brother Karl, who was studying at the art school on the same street.

Schubert would also go into the city for his lessons with Salieri, and he still sometimes participated in the musical life of the Seminary.

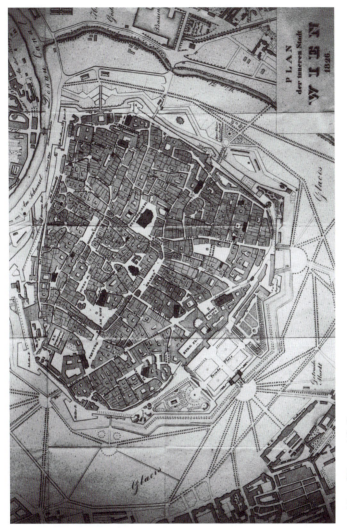

5 Map of Vienna (1826).

Since many friends remained there throughout their university studies, Schubert often visited on Sunday and on holidays. In purely quantitative terms, these years were the most productive of Schubert's life, and he could always share new compositions. In December 1814, Schubert wrote the first movement of his Second Symphony, which he finished in March of the following year and dedicated to Franz Innocenz Lang, the Seminary's director, who had created their orchestra.

Schubert's student years span a particularly eventful period in Vienna's political history. The climate became increasingly repressive, a striking contrast to the Enlightenment ideals Mozart had enjoyed under Emperor Joseph II. Beethoven's dreams of a freer society found expression early in a cantata commemorating the Emperor's death in 1790 and ultimately in his Ninth Symphony some thirty-four years later. For those who remembered the remarkable reforms of the 1780s – the political and religious liberalization, the growth of education and health care – the first decades of the new century must have seemed increasingly gloomy.

An early memory of Schubert's would have been the invasion of Napoleon's army in 1805 and a second occupation in 1809, which Spaun vividly recalled years later:

> On the evening of 12 May, at 9 o'clock, the bombardment of the city began. It was a magnificent sight to see the glowing cannonballs curving across the night sky, while the many conflagrations reddened the sky. Before our very eyes a ball from a howitzer fell in the University square and burst on one of the lovely fountains there; but all of a sudden there was a crash in the house itself, a howitzer shell having fallen on the building. It penetrated every floor down to the first. (SMF 353)

By 1814, the year Schubert composed his first great songs, the city was hosting the Congress of Vienna, convened to divide up Europe in the aftermath of Napoleon's defeat. The fateful decisions of this "congress that danced" would last until mid century, solidifying a repressive regime under Prince Clemens von Metternich which would affect Schubert in ways both large and small for the rest of his life. While comparisons to modern totalitarian regimes would be exaggerated, nevertheless suspicion, censorship, and constraints were daily realities during Schubert's time. From political repression, rampant inflation, and pervasive restrictions, to diet, health, and means of earning a livelihood, Schubert dealt with considerable hardships – circumstances, to be sure, that were in no way unique to him, but which nonetheless profoundly affected his life and art.

Schubert's return home after the Seminary meant that he was once again living near a childhood friend, Therese Grob (1798–1875), who has long been identified as his "first youthful passion" (SMF 59). Any love letters Schubert may have written during his lifetime have disappeared, nor are there unambiguous references to romantic relationships in surviving correspondence or other writings. Schubert's love life has long fascinated posterity. Until recently, he was typically portrayed as extremely interested in attractive young women, even if his infatuations typically proved unsuccessful. From this sentimental and pathetic image, recent speculations about Schubert's possible homosexuality are quite a remarkable revision.

The teenage relationship with Therese demands special attention as she is the first of two women (the other is Countess Caroline Esterházy) about whom there is both limited contemporaneous and retrospective information that suggests some impassioned feelings. Schubert's family was extremely close to the Grobs. They lived nearby, the parents were friends (and sometimes god-parents to each other's children). Their offspring came together frequently, and eventually Ignaz Schubert married Therese's aunt. Therese's father, a respectable silk merchant, died in 1804, and his widow lived relatively comfortably until her death in 1826. Education and music frequently brought the families together and, we might guess, the Grobs' home offered more comfortable surroundings than did the Schuberts' in which to socialize and make music. (For one thing, the Grobs must have had a piano; the Schuberts supposedly acquired one only late in 1814.) According to information Kreissle obtained from the Grob family, "Schubert was like an adopted son in the house."[8]

Therese, who was nearly two years younger than Schubert, possessed an exceptional, light soprano voice that by every account enchanted him. Her brother Heinrich (1800–55) was likewise an accomplished musician, especially as a pianist and organist, though he also played violin and cello. Schubert often made music at the Grobs', activities which proved to be a particularly important creative outlet during his adolescence. Anton Holzapfel, who knew both families at the time, attests that these encounters were "certainly not without influence on his first works, as the Grob household was given to serious music-making" (SMF 60).

Throughout his life Schubert had a remarkable ability to capture the emotions of a feminine persona and express them in song. Some of these earliest achievements were probably inspired by Therese, who surely sang them for him. Schubert gave at least sixteen songs to her, three of which survive only in her collection.[9] Perhaps not too much should be made of these songs, which are often referred to as an album; they were written on loose manuscript pages, all but one in Schubert's hand. None of them dates later than 1816, when Therese was just turning eighteen, and only a few deal with love themes. In any case, Schubert often gave songs to his friends, and he apparently wrote at least one piece for Heinrich Grob (D487).

Did Schubert fall in love with the Therese's winning personality, with her young body, with her angelic voice, with the enjoyable domestic evenings of convivial music-making, or with some combination of these attractions? Anselm Hüttenbrenner recalls Schubert's telling him that Therese "was not exactly pretty and her face had pockmarks; but she had a heart, a heart of gold" (SMF 182). Holzapfel describes her as "by no means a beauty but she was well built, rather plump and with a fresh, childlike round little face; she had a lovely soprano voice"; he characterizes Schubert's feelings as "violent," if probably "unrequited" (SMF 62, 59). He further relates that Schubert confessed to him his love for Therese in a letter which he later lost, and that he "ridiculously tried to dissuade [Schubert] from this passion" in a long letter (SMF 61). If Schubert had wished to marry Therese, he would have encountered difficulties because of a law decreed in 1815 that required proof of sufficient income.[10]

Hüttenbrenner provides an account of the course of this putative romance: the two were attracted to one another, "she won his heart because she sang a soprano solo so well in [his] Mass [in F]," but as they were young and Schubert too poor, she obeyed her father by marrying another. "From that time," Hüttenbrenner announces, Schubert "had a dominating aversion to the daughters of Eve" and so long as he knew him there was "not even the suspicion of a love affair" (SMF 70; cf. 182). While these recollections are undoubtedly valuable, we should remember that Hüttenbrenner did not know Therese or even her name, that Therese's father was in no position to object to the marriage as he was long since dead, and that Hüttenbrenner's information about this romance came some four decades after the fact, as did Holzapfel's. Their testimony is the sole information available about this romantic relationship. Ferdinand Schubert, who knew the entire Grob family well, and who wrote his reminiscences much closer in time to the events, simply referred to Schubert's "good friend and his favorite singer" (SMF 36), and although Therese lived a long life, dying at age 76, she never mentioned any romance with the famous Franz Schubert. Therese talked to Kreissle but, perhaps out of discretion, or even regret, gave no details besides the closeness of the families making music together; she cherished the songs Schubert gave her for the rest of her life.

To this day, some immortalize Therese Grob as Schubert's only love, a woman who sadly left him broken-hearted to marry a master baker, and on whose account Schubert renounced marriage (or, according to Hüttenbrenner, shunned women entirely). This all seems highly unlikely, more the stuff of the novels which this teenage relationship eventually spawned than an accurate portrait of Schubert's early emotional life. Furthermore, it is striking that the comments by Holzapfel, Hüttenbrenner, Ferdinand Schubert, and even by Therese herself through Kreissle, all specifically mention that Schubert's feelings were intimately connected with her performing his music – she was his *Lieblings-Sängerin*. If we can say she inspired Schubert, it was not just in Lieder, but also in religious music that suited her voice. In Schubert's limited experience thus far, family friend Therese Grob might best be considered the first significant interpreter of his music, the one who brought his most accomplished works to life and who transformed the silent sounds of his inner ear into living music all could enjoy.

The performance of Schubert's Mass in F (D105) in which, according to Hüttenbrenner, Therese "won Schubert's heart," was a particularly momentous occasion for him because it might be considered his professional debut as a composer. The performance commemorated the centennial of the Lichtental Church in September 1814. Ferdinand Schubert played the organ, Michael Holzer prepared the choir, Therese sang the soprano solo, violin virtuoso Joseph Mayseder served as concertmaster, and Schubert conducted. Salieri supposedly attended this, his student's first public success. Vienna was given a glimpse of a remarkable new talent. Ferdinand asserts that a second performance took place ten days later at the more prestigious St. Augustine's Court Church, before an audience that would no doubt have included foreign dignitaries attending the Congress of Vienna.

Reviews document neither event, yet the attention may have made Schubert even more determined on his course as a composer. If Ferdinand's report is accurate, Schubert may, at least temporarily, even won over his father, who reportedly presented him with a five-octave Graf piano (SMF 36). The Mass in F signaled the start of a new phase in Schubert's career. What is more remarkable is that some two weeks later he composed his first masterpiece, a work that forever changed the stature of an entire genre.

3 Ingenious Schubert: "The prince of song"

[Vogl's] bold performance [of Erlkönig] broke down the barriers for
the simple and modest master, and presented the new prince of song
to the capital.

Albert Stadler, 1853 (SMF 215)

Few adolescent composers' works are heard as frequently today as are
Schubert's. Posterity marvels at Mozart's precocious juvenile exploits
and yet largely ignores his early compositions. Mendelssohn's teenage works number among his greatest, but those in the concert repertory remain relatively few. The youthful Schubert did not display
prodigious gifts comparable to Mozart's and Mendelssohn's, nor did
he cause any similar public sensation. Indeed, Schubert attracted little
attention at all until 1820, his twenty-third year, by which time he had
already composed two-thirds of his total oeuvre. Yet dozens of these
early compositions eventually achieved repertory status.

The principal impetus for the retrospective discovery of Schubert's
charming early symphonies, as well as of his string quartets, Masses,
and works in a variety of other genres, was the prestige of the extraordinary songs he wrote as a teenager. With some exaggeration we
might say that Schubert elevated the Lied to worthy and respectable
status, while at the same time Lieder opened doors, aroused curiosity,
made him famous, and secured his place in music history. In the 1820s
and 1830s, references to him, no matter the context, usually used the

6 Cover of the second edition of Schubert's first famous work: Erlkönig, Op. 1.

label "the Lied composer Franz Schubert." (Other catch phrases alluded, as in the case of Mozart, to his genius and early death.) Some writers simply tagged Schubert as the "composer of Erlkönig," for long his single most famous work, and by mid century he was crowned as the Liederfürst ("Prince of Song").

Schubert had already written dozens of songs, as well as pieces in the significant instrumental, keyboard, dramatic, and sacred genres, by the time he composed his first indisputable masterpiece, Gretchen am Spinnrade, on 19 October 1814. His helpful precision in dating the manuscript has provided a convenient, if somewhat misleading, designation: the "birthdate of the German Lied." Composers, of course, had been writing songs for centuries. What changed dramatically during the nineteenth century, largely because of Schubert, was the importance and significance of what had previously been considered a minor musical genre. Schubert's immediate predecessors, such as Johann Rudolph Zumsteeg, Johann Friedrich Reichardt, and Carl Friedrich Zelter, wrote highly praised Lieder, but they neither elevated the stature of genre nor artistically surpassed the best songs of Mozart and Beethoven.

Critics and historians began to take Lieder more seriously during Schubert's lifetime. Lengthy reviews of his latest productions would sometimes begin with the comment that such attention was unusual but warranted for this particular composer. Appropriately, all of Schubert's first publications were songs. More than two decades earlier, at a comparable stage in his own career, Beethoven had honored his larger chamber and keyboard compositions by assigning them opus numbers. Likewise Schubert, in his debut publications, crowned his Lieder with opus numbers, signaling that they too were significant works of substantial content.

Robert Schumann regarded the Lied as "the only genre in which a remarkable improvement has occurred since Beethoven's time," a progress enhanced by "a new German school of poetry."[1] For Schubert, Goethe's poetry in particular inspired his earliest masterpieces, not only Gretchen and Erlkönig, but also Heidenröslein, Rastlose

Liebe, and many other songs. While it may not be surprising that
Schubert set Goethe's poems more often than any other (he was, after
all, Germany's greatest living lyric poet), his interest came mainly in
the early years; after 1822 he rarely turned to Goethe (or to Schiller).
Other factors contributed to the flowering of the Lied in the early nineteenth century: the Romantic cultivation of small-scale forms in
general (the very idea of promoting a four-minute composition as a
masterpiece was foreign to the Baroque and Classical eras); the robust
middle-class musical culture and widespread domestic music-
making; and the new tonal qualities and technical capacities of the
piano. Before Schubert, song melodies and accompaniments were
usually fairly simple, and a singer would often play for himself or herself at the piano. Improvements in piano construction served
Schubert's interpretive goals magnificently: thrilling keyboard parts
of unprecedented intensity, extraordinary difficulty, and unifying
power were newly possible.

Beginning with his earliest songs, Schubert used material phe-
nomena as metaphors for psychological states of mind. A spinning
wheel in *Gretchen* and a ride through a storm in *Erlkönig* are represented
in perpetual motion keyboard accompaniments, a relentless invoca-
tion of unease and anxiety. Such procedures express more than mere
descriptive tone painting of a realistic element in the poem – they
convey the dominant mood of the literary text. No single trait defines
Schubert's achievement or innovation in the Lied, for there is a complex alchemy of ravishing lyricism, moving declamation, harmonic
ingenuity, a true partnership of voice and piano, and psychological
penetration into the texts that function differently in each song. What
is remarkable about Schubert is that these traits were all there from
the beginning, from at least age seventeen, and only deepened over
the next fourteen years.

In 1815 alone, Schubert composed nearly 150 songs, though not a
single one had yet been published, performed in public, or mentioned
in the press. As his Lieder poured forth, they circulated widely in manuscript copies among admirers. Friends, principally from the

Seminary, served not only as Schubert's audience (and also preserva-
tionists – many survive solely in their hand-written copies), but also as
collaborators in that they often provided texts or steered him toward
poets otherwise unknown to him. In so doing, friends helped supple-
ment Schubert's rather conservative general education.

In eighteen years, from 1810 to 1828, Schubert wrote roughly 630
Lieder that set the words of more than one hundred different poets.
(Sometimes he would return to set the same poem again, either as a
minor revision or as a wholesale reconception.) Schubert used some
sources only once or twice, but there are seventy-four Goethe and
forty-four Schiller settings. He turned to poems, in German translation, by the ancient Greeks, by Shakespeare and other English poets,
by Italians, and also turned to major and minor German poets of the
eighteenth and early nineteenth century. Schubert frequently chose
poems written by those he knew personally. Johann Baptist
Mayrhofer, with whom he lived for nearly two years, received the most
attention with forty-seven, and there are songs to texts by Bauernfeld,
Bruchmann, Kenner, Anton Ottenwalt, Schober, Senn, Spaun, and
Albert Stadler, as well as acquaintances such as Castelli, Matthäus von
Collin, Grillparzer, Körner, Karoline Pichler, Johann Ladislaus
Pyrker, and others. The breadth of the poetry, the range of the musical
emotions explored, the length and structure of songs, and their rela-
tive simplicity or complexity not only set the standards of the genre for
later composers, but also have yet to be surpassed.[2]

As this wealth of music was pouring forth, Schubert also had to
attend to more mundane concerns. Although a "bad" (*schlecht*) grade
in religion marred his record at the k. k. Normalhauptschule, he nevertheless passed the qualification examination in August 1814 and
joined his brothers teaching at their father's school. He was the sixth
assistant, the lowest level, and responsible for instructing the young-
est children; he also gave some private music lessons. Friends and
family relate that Schubert lacked the requisite interest and patience
for this profession. Mayrhofer states in his 1829 memorial to
Schubert:

[Schubert was] an assistant teacher, a hard lot, time-wasting, arduous, and on the whole thankless, for my youthful, aspiring friend, whose life lay in melody. I believe this was the source of the aversion to music teaching which he expressed later. But the art of music and the interest of a few friends may have consoled and fortified him in such a depressing situation. (SDB 861)

However onerous his teaching duties, circumstances were not so dispiriting as to distract him from creating his initial masterpieces or to keep him from slowly receiving some public exposure. Indeed, as Mayrhofer tells us, music was Schubert's salvation.

Gradually, the focus of Schubert's musical world shifted from reading through chamber music and orchestral works with family and friends at home and at the Seminary to larger gatherings with more mature amateur and professional musicians. He played in what might be considered a community orchestra, which grew so much that it had to keep moving to larger quarters, at first in the home of the merchant Franz Frischling, and eventually to the apartment of one Otto Hatwig, a musician at the Burg-Theater, in the Gundelhof. Schubert was a violist, Ferdinand and Heinrich Grob played violin, and the group became large enough to tackle symphonies by Haydn, Mozart, and Beethoven. At Hatwig's Schubert also heard some of his own overtures and symphonies, such as the Fifth in B-flat (D485), which was played in the fall 1816. Leopold von Sonnleithner much later described these musical events in some detail and listed thirty-five members by name; "apart from a few professional musicians, most of the gentlemen belonged to the merchant-tradesman or minor official class" (SMF 340).

In Schubert's personal life, as well, the center of gravity switched from his own family and family friends, such as the Grobs, to the new group of friends he had lived with at the Seminary or met through them. Many of these figures remained steadfast until his death. They were the ones, such as Spaun and Schober, to whom Schubert wrote group letters when he made his first trip away from Vienna in 1818. Here he addressed his "dearest and best friends" and declared that they were "everything" to him (SDB 93). In recent years, scholars have discovered a good deal more information about the activities of Schubert's close friends and acquaintances during the 1810s. Musicologist David Gramit, among others, has examined the intellectual and artistic tenets of those hailing from Linz who exerted the dominant aesthetic and moral influence on Schubert at this time.[3] They included not only Spaun, but also Spaun's brother Anton, and Anton Ottenwalt, who in 1819 married their sister Marie (she had previously been courted by Schober). Bruchmann, Kenner, Mayrhofer, Schober, and Senn had all moved from Linz, and many knew one another from their days at the Kremsmünster Seminary. These Linz friends were typically a bit older than Schubert, came from richer, more prominent families, and by the time Schubert met them had already formed quite strong views on how to live a proper life.

This "Bildung Circle" (the concept of *Bildung*, so valued in nineteenth-century German culture, denotes self-improvement through education) had clearly stated objectives, held regular meetings, and even produced a short-lived periodical, *Beyträge zur Bildung für Jünglinge* (Contributions to the Cultivation of Youth), to promote their intellectual and aesthetic program. A letter from Anton von Spaun to Schober captures some of the core beliefs of the Linz circle, and also offers further hints that Schober's virtue and laziness required constant monitoring:

> We must study humanity, and all ages, and what the best people of
> the past did and thought, and how one thing leads to another, and
> how one thing follows out of another, so that we can understand
> clearly and have a positive influence on the people we love, on our
> brothers. Beauty, too, influences human hearts powerfully,
> refreshingly, and upliftingly, and the sounds of music, a Madonna by
> Raphael, an Apollo, the song of a divinely inspired poet, all pull
> heavenward with an unknown power; therefore let us, too, dedicate
> our lives and flee nothing so much as an excess of destructive
> passions and the deficiency and emptiness of an indolent spirit.[4]

Schubert's friends furnished much of the artistic support he needed, the poetry he now encountered that inspired his first masterpieces, and the values and ideals he internalized. The notion that a brotherhood imbued with a "common love of the good" could actively ennoble and benefit society through art and ideas must have completely won over Schubert. No matter his superior creative genius, Schubert was at a tender and impressionable age. He benefited in many ways from associating with passionate young men, older and of higher social rank, who believed in his gifts. They gave him guidance, introduced him to people and situations he might otherwise not have encountered, provided him with material goods and lodging, acquainted him with a vast spectrum of greatness in all of the arts – and they did this in the conviction that the importance of their project was something bigger than mere pleasure or self-indulgent satisfaction. These remarkably cultured and intelligent individuals, although musically sophisticated and passionate, were not professional musicians themselves. By training and inclination, they were literary and artistic, hence their natural preoccupation with Schubert's Lieder and their frequent lack of understanding of his larger instrumental works and of his purely musical accomplishments. While they furthered the literary knowledge and sensibilities crucial to Schubert's song compositions, they have been blamed for diverting him from a more traditionally rigorous musical education.

Schubert's Linz friends placed a particularly high value on industriousness, and as a consequence there are frequent allusions in letters to Schubert's amazing productivity, as well as to Schober's idleness. One of Schubert's nicknames was "Canevas," from "Kann er was?" (Can he do anything?), the question he would inevitably ask when someone new entered the picture. The circle was a meritocracy of sorts in which each had to prove his worth. Bauernfeld tells us that Schubert "suffered from a genuine dread of commonplace and boring people, of philistines, whether from the upper or middle classes . . . Goethe's cry 'I would rather die than be bored' was and remained his motto" (SMF 230).

Schubert met Schober soon after the latter moved to Vienna in 1815 and he remained central to Schubert's life until the very end. The friendship with Spaun also flourished during the periods they were both living in Vienna. Yet many of the individuals in the early Linz circle had little contact with Schubert during the 1820s. A new group ascended, again united by deep artistic and intellectual passions. The earlier Linz circle and the later Vienna friends often overlapped, particularly because of Spaun and Schober; Schubertiades at Spaun's home in the late 1820s comprised many common participants. In addition, Schubert visited Linz in 1819, 1823, and 1825.

In this regard, we must consider that although Vienna's population (some 290,000 in 1824) was large for its day (only London, Paris, and Constantinople were bigger), the social class in which Schubert circulated was limited. Approximately 50,000 lived in the inner city. The nobility and wealthy bourgeoisie inhabited a realm Schubert rarely entered, while the mass of humanity lived at a quite miserable level of subsistence. Schubert's social sphere of upper-middle class officials and civil servants generally shared similar educational backgrounds, political views, and a common quality of life. At times it seems that Schubert knew everyone worth knowing in Vienna's intellectual and artistic spheres, but then it appears that they all knew one another.

Schubert was introduced to some prominent young men, primarily literary figures, actors, and artists, through a club, the Unsinnsgesellschaft (Nonsense Society), which met in 1817–18. Schubert, it appears, was its sole professional musician, although not one of the original members. Musicologist Rita Steblin has uncovered evidence of Schubert's participation in this fascinating group and closely examined twenty-nine surviving issues of their weekly newsletter, the *Archiv des menschlichen Unsinns* (Archive of Human Nonsense).[5] Handwritten and often superbly illustrated, they show a far less high-minded purpose than did the journal of the Bildung Circle. Indeed, the conviviality, good fun, and silliness of this irreverent society diverge strikingly from the earnestness of the Linz group and point more toward Schubert's future. Artistic interests were the common denominator of these otherwise different circles, although Schubert's allegiances gradually changed from the anti-Romanticism and censorious moralism typical of his Linz friends to the more progressive, "Bohemian" sensibility of the practicing painters, poets, and theater people with whom he increasingly spent his time.

"Today I composed for money for first time," Schubert wrote on 17 June 1816. He had been commissioned to compose the cantata *Prometheus* to celebrate the name-day of Professor Heinrich Josef Watteroth, a popular scholar and music lover with whom Spaun was lodging at the time. The lengthy composition for soprano, bass, chorus, and orchestra was lost during Schubert's lifetime; only a few melodies remain, remembered decades later by Sonnleithner. Some of Schubert's friends participated in the performance, which he himself conducted, and one of them subsequently wrote a poem "To Herr Franz Schubert," which appeared a year later in the *Wiener Allgemeine Theaterzeitung*. This was the first mention of Schubert in the press, a versified tribute that seems symbolically appropriate for a composer who made his reputation with the Lied (SDB 79–80).

In addition to writing more songs in 1815 than at any other time in his life, Schubert also composed many dances. Over the years, Schubert wrote down hundreds of them and he must have improvised countless more at Schubertiades and at other social gatherings. His Ländler, galops, marches, ecossaisses, Deutsche, and minuets display a wide array of styles and moods, not to mention tempi, meters, and keys. Schubert usually wrote them for piano, solo or duet, although he composed some for strings, and many others were anonymously arranged for other instruments or were orchestrated. As in his songs, Schubert's bold harmonic explorations in brief dances are far less conventional than his instrumental works of the same period. One can conceive of Schubert's writing these smaller works while juggling teaching duties, but that he also composed four Singspiele (German operettas) at the same time is unexpected: *Der vierjährige*

Posten, Fernando (to a libretto by Stadler), Claudine von Villa Bella (unfinished, and later partly destroyed), and Die Freunde von Salamanka. In
this same phenomenally productive year, Schubert wrote his Second
and Third Masses (D167, 324), finished his Second Symphony (D125),
and began the Third (D200). The amazing pace continued the following year with nearly one hundred songs, the Fourth and Fifth
Symphonies (D417, 485), the Mass in C (D452), an unfinished opera,
Die Bürgschaft, and numerous chamber works, including the violin
sonatinas (D384, 385, 408).

Such creative productivity must have been at odds with the drudgery of his teaching job and what we may reasonably guess were more
than occasional conflicts with a stern and pious father keen on social
respectability. Schubert lived briefly with Spaun in the home of
Watteroth in the spring of 1816, and it was during this time that he sent
in a late application for a position teaching music at the German
Normal School in Laibach (now Ljubljana in Slovenia), some two hundred miles south of Vienna. Some scholars feel the immediate impetus for his suit was the desire to make enough money so as to satisfy
the "Marriage Consent Law" and thus be able to marry Therese Grob.
It should be noted, however, that none of Schubert's brothers or
friends married so early in life (Schubert had just turned nineteen and
Therese was seventeen); in fact, late marriages were far more
common.

Schubert's assessment of his qualifications for the Laibach job, as
well as the recommendations of those who supported his petition,
give some measure of his stature at nineteen. Although by this age, the
musical gifts of Mozart, Beethoven, and Rossini had received wide
recognition, Schubert – so far as the Viennese public was concerned –
had not yet accomplished anything exceptional and no special claims
could be made on his behalf. Indeed, that Schubert composed at all is
barely mentioned in the application process. Schubert lists three principal qualifications: first, his musical education (at the Seminary, as a
choirboy in the Imperial Court Chapel, and under the guidance of
Salieri); second, his abilities "in all branches of composition, in

performance on the organ and violin, and in singing" has led to him being declared "the most suitable among all the applicants for this post"; last, his promise to do a good job. Salieri's letter of recommendation, written in Italian (after fifty years in Vienna he still had not mastered German), may not come across as a ringing endorsement, but it was intended simply to convey that he had interviewed the candidates, considered Schubert the best among them, and therefore found it unnecessary for him to take an examination to confirm his musical abilities: "I, the undersigned, assert that I support the application of Franz Schubert" (SDB 54). In the end, one of the other twenty-one applicants got the job, and Schubert remained in Vienna.

Although Schubert apparently continued to teach, at least intermittently, at his father's school until the summer of 1818, he took a further step toward independence near the end of 1816 by temporarily moving in with Schober and his family (his mother and younger sister) in the inner city. It was soon thereafter that Schober made the crucial introduction to Vogl. Among Schubert's famous songs from 1817 are Der Tod und das Mädchen, Die Forelle, Ganymed, and An die Musik. During the summer Schubert immersed himself in writing piano sonatas, not all of which he completed. By fall 1817, Schubert had returned to his family home, and late that year his father was promoted to a better school district in the Rossau suburb, slightly closer to the inner city. Schubert lived with his parents that winter until the chance arose for another departure, this time for his first excursion from Vienna. There are some hints in letters from the time that Schubert would not, perhaps could not, go back home when he returned. Possibly Schubert forced a real break with teaching, if not with his family, so that he might concentrate more on composition; the phrase Spaun used often was a "life dedicated to art."

For more than four months in the summer and early fall of 1818, Schubert secured a temporary, though well-paying, job. Count Johann Carl Esterházy engaged the twenty-one-year-old composer to teach his two daughters, Marie, age fifteen, and Caroline, age twelve. While the instruction would later continue in Vienna, Schubert's initial assignment was to accompany the family to their country estate in Zseliz, Hungary, on the Gran river (now Želiezovce in Slovakia), some hundred miles east of Vienna. In a letter home, Schubert observed that "our castle is not one of the largest, but very neatly built and it is surrounded by a most beautiful garden" and described the large cast of characters living at the castle of the Esterházy family: "The count is rather rough, the countess haughty but more sensitive; the young countesses are nice children." Among a list of servants and employees, he mentions a chambermaid, "very pretty and often [his] companion." Deutsch identifies her as Josefine ("Pepi") Pöckelhofer, and there are hints of some affair between them, although the evidence is slight – Schubert, for instance, refers to an estate manager as his "rival" (SDB 98–100; cf. 362, 371).

The chance to quit his teaching job and leave Vienna for the first time must have proved extremely attractive, especially as living conditions declined precipitously during the hot summer months. Anyone with the means sought to flee the city's dust and foul air and head to more pleasant – and more hygienic – locations. While the greatest legacy of Schubert's various excursions in this and later summers is the music he composed in carefree natural surroundings, a secondary benefit is the letters he wrote home to family and friends. Indeed, except for the few surviving diary entries, these letters provide unusual access to Schubert's own voice and attitudes. (Most of his other substantial letters were either connected with business or written to friends who were themselves traveling.)

The initial freedom Schubert experienced in Zseliz proved intoxicating: "I live and compose like a god, as if it should always be so," he wrote to Schober and Company some three weeks after arriving. He considered his recent setting of Mayrhofer's *Einsamkeit* the best thing he had composed because he was "*without* a care," and he made a telling remark concerning the urgency of his escape from Vienna: "Thank God I live at last, and it was high time, otherwise I should have been nothing but a thwarted musician" (SDB 93). Ignaz Schubert, back in Vienna, back with father, was still ensconced in the drudgery of teaching. He freely expressed his delight, tinged with envy, at his brother's good fortune:

> You happy creature! How enviable is your lot! You live in sweet golden freedom, can give free reign to your musical genius, can allow your thoughts stray where they will; you are loved, admired, idolized, while the likes of us wretched scholastic beasts of burden are abandoned to all the roughness of wild youngsters and exposed to a host of abuses, not to mention that we are subjected to the further humiliation of an ungrateful public and a lot of dunderheaded bigwigs.

Ignaz alludes to some tough times at home, where no one dares laugh when he tells an amusing story concerning "superstition in religious education." Schubert is "now free of all these things" (SDB 103).

Whereas Schubert's correspondence with Ignaz reveals something of their shared attitude toward organized religion and pompous clergy, as well as toward the constricted atmosphere in which they grew up, Franz Theodor's letters are filled with conventional pieties and constant talk of God. Six years later, when Schubert again returned to Zseliz, his father wrote to him, "It is my daily prayer to God that He may enlighten and strengthen me and mine, that we may ever become more worthy of His goodwill and His blessings" (SDB 368); many of his letters exhibit a similar tone. The one he wrote to Ferdinand the day Schubert died takes comfort in religion while saying nothing about his son. The Schubert children were clearly raised in a strict and religiously observant home and, one may reasonably surmise, a fairly oppressive one. Ignaz had concluded his letter, quoted above, "If you should wish to write to Papa and me at the same time, do not touch upon any religious matters."

Schubert's own religious views are more difficult to define.[6] He composed six complete Latin Masses, and part of an oratorio, as well as numerous smaller sacred works. While in Zseliz, he wrote a German Requiem (D621) for Ferdinand – not, fortunately, because his brother had died, but rather because Ferdinand sometimes passed off his brother's compositions as his own to enhance a modest career as a composer. "Your German Requiem is finished. It made me sad, believe me, for I sang it from the depth of my soul," Schubert wrote Ferdinand in August; some years later, Ferdinand would publish the piece under his own name as his Op. 2 (SDB 94). During a trip to Upper Austria in 1825, he wrote to his parents concerning the Lied *Ellens Gesang III*, which "seems to touch all hearts, and inspires a feeling of devotion. I believe the reason is that I never force myself to be devout, and never compose hymns or prayers of that sort except when the mood takes me; but then it is usually the right and true devotion" (SDB 435). This song, better known as *Ave Maria*, eventually became one of Schubert's most famous; unfortunately, the victim of its own success, it was endlessly trivialized in gushing performances and kitsch arrangements.

The depth of Schubert's feelings when writing *Ave Maria*, the great pantheistic song *Die Allmacht*, and other select works touching on spiritual matters, is profound. In general, however, liturgical pieces, for all the wonderful moments in his Masses, prove more problematic. Schubert was nurtured in a great tradition of sacred music; moreover, professional opportunities arose from writing church music that helped advance his career. Yet even though composers at the time often omitted small sections of the Mass text, the fact that Schubert consistently expunged the lines from the Credo pledging fealty to the Catholic Church and belief in the resurrection of the dead indicates some resistance to formal religious dogma, whether encountered at home, in school (Schubert's one unsatisfactory grade), or in church. In 1827, in jest, a friend began a letter by writing out a musical incipit over the words "Credo in unum Deum!" followed by the exclamation, "Not you, I know well enough" (SDB 597).

After a while, the glow of his idyllic existence in Zseliz began to fade. Schubert's first letters had told of how happy he was and how kind the people were, but he later complained that "not a soul here has any feeling for true art." To Ferdinand he amplified: "Had I not, day by day, gotten to know the people around me better, things would be as well with me as at the beginning. But now I see that I am alone among them after all" (SDB 99, 109). Nevertheless, Schubert continued his association with the Esterházy family and returned to Zseliz for an even longer stay in 1824. Throughout his time away, Schubert's thoughts were very much of his friends and of Vienna: "Well and happy as I am here, and kind as the people are, I look forward with immense pleasure to the moment where the word will be 'To Vienna, to Vienna!'" Near the end of his stay, he wrote, "My longing for Vienna grows daily" (SDB 95, 109). Ignaz expressed his fear that when Schubert got back to Vienna his "new circumstances" – that is, living in the center of the city, surrounded by sophisticated friends – would rarely allow him to see his family, and that this would inevitably distance him from the grim life of the schoolmaster.

Indeed, Schubert did not return home after Zseliz, but rather moved in with Mayrhofer, with whom he shared a room in the inner city until the end of 1820. The poet was someone, unconnected to the Seminary, who entered Schubert's life through the Linz circle and quickly emerged an important influence, both personal and artistic. They met in 1814 when Spaun gave a poem written by his old friend (and former roommate), "Am See," to Schubert for him to set to music. Mayrhofer was ten years older than the composer, sophisticated and well educated, prone to severe melancholy, and, though politically liberal, employed as a government book censor. In 1836, after two unsuccessful attempts, he committed suicide by jumping out of his office window. Mayrhofer provided an environment of which Schubert's father could grudgingly approve. As he recalled in his 1829 tribute to Schubert, "I often had to console Schubert's worthy father about his son's future, and I dared to prophesy that Franz would surely prevail, nay that a later world would give him his due, slowly though it came to him at first" (SMF 14).

As we shall see in the next chapter, Schubert completed far fewer compositions during the five or so years after he left home. His song output dropped precipitously, from more than a hundred a year to only one or two dozen. He stopped composing larger instrumental pieces almost entirely – no completed quartets or symphonies, and a prolonged genesis for the Mass in A-flat (D678) – although he did pursue some theater projects, including *Die Zwillingsbrüder* and the unfinished *Adrast*. Notable exceptions were keyboard compositions and the "Trout" Quintet (D667). The quintet likely dates from 1819 when Schubert traveled with Vogl to the singer's birthplace in Upper Austria. This was the first of three extended summer journeys which Schubert made with the singer, who probably assumed many of the expenses. In Steyr, a wealthy music patron and amateur cellist named Sylvester Paumgartner, who had been delighted by Schubert's song *Die Forelle*, apparently asked him to include the melody in a chamber work. Schubert based the fourth movement on the earlier song, casting it as a set of variations on the vocal part; he brought in the song's rippling piano accompaniment only at the end. During this trip Schubert also probably wrote his Piano Sonata in A Major (D664), another one of his sunniest works.

In both the summers Schubert spent in Zseliz he composed a large quantity of four-hand piano music. Before 1818 he had written relatively little in this intimate format, but given that he was teaching piano and entertaining the Esterházy family, the attraction of the piano duet is clear. For the rest of his life Schubert continued to pursue this medium; no composer before or after created such substantial and compelling four-hand pieces. Their gradual loss of popularity (as with Schubert's many glorious partsongs) is one result of the general decline in domestic music-making. Among the works he wrote the first summer are a four-hand Sonata in B flat (D617), a set of variations, Op. 10 (D624), which he dedicated to Beethoven, and the popular Military Marches (D733).

As the decade drew to a close and with Schubert now in his early twenties, his professional career was slowly beginning to advance. Even before the first trip to Zseliz, his name had started to appear rather frequently in the Viennese press and, more sporadically, in foreign periodicals. The song *Erlafsee* appeared in an artistic almanac,

7 "Michael Vogl and Franz Schubert Marching to Battle and Victory," pencil caricature by Franz von Schober (?).

which, although not a high-profile publication, did at least begin the process of getting pieces released. (*Widerschein* and *Die Forelle* were also issued early on in similar unassuming venues.) The first truly public performance of a secular Schubert composition was advertised in the *Wiener Allgemeine Theaterzeitung* in late February 1818 as "An entirely new Overture by Herr Franz Schubert." The work was unanimously praised in both Viennese and foreign papers, which identified the composer as a student of Salieri. The early reviews of Schubert's music often commented on qualities praised in his music ever since: Schubert knows "how to touch and stir all hearts. Although the theme [of the overture] was surprisingly simple, a wealth of the most astonishing and agreeable ideas developed from it, worked out with vigor and skill" (SDB 87).

The public première of a Schubert Lied, *Schäfers Klagelied*, in March 1819, prompted further enthusiastic comment: "A beautiful composition," a "sensitive setting of Goethe's poem" (SDB 116). The song also attracted a foreign review, in the Berlin *Gesellschafter*, which hailed it as "most enjoyable . . . we look forward to a larger work by this promising artist" (SDB 115). Schubert's first notices in the press were nearly all as positive and encouraging. Poised for greater public recognition, Schubert now entered a period of overwhelming personal and creative turmoil.

4 Popular Schubert: "The turning point"

1820 – this date constitutes a turning point [in Schubert's career],
namely the first public appearance of his works.

Leopold von Sonnleithner, 1857 (SMF 118)

One of the most durable of Schubert myths concerns the neglect he
allegedly suffered at the hands of an indifferent public. Only faithful
friends, so the story goes, appreciated his true worth and actively supported his art. Schubert is cast as the unrecognized creative genius,
whose real accomplishment was discovered too late, long after his far
too early death. As with many legends, this misleading image does, in
fact, register significant realities of Schubert's unusual career. Some
noteworthy features of his reputation come into clearer focus when
we consider the unfolding of his compositional and professional
activities within their contemporary context. Was Schubert's music
really so neglected during his lifetime? What opportunities were available to him? And what was the true extent of his public fame at the time
of his death?

In truth, Schubert's situation was both better and worse than myth
would have it. While the public appreciated a large quantity of his
music, few, even among his supportive friends, knew the full reach of
his artistic accomplishment. Schubert was one of the most widely
published and performed composers active in Vienna during the
1820s. Reviews and advertisements often referred to him as a "popu-

lar composer" (beliebter Tonsetzer), but the pieces that made him beloved were limited primarily to the relatively unprestigious Lied and other genres that did even less to enhance his stature – dances, part-songs, and short piano pieces. The symphonies, operas, religious and chamber music that would normally have launched and sustained a major reputation – that would have made him a "great" composer – were generally unknown until his last years and were, even then, still quite unrepresentative in relation to the actual scope of what he had composed.

Even a friend as close as Spaun was not altogether informed about the very real discrepancy between the pieces known in Vienna during the 1820s and Schubert's phenomenal compositional legacy. Like the general public, Schubert's friends too viewed him primarily as a Lied composer. Spaun admitted as much himself privately in an 1829 letter: "For all the admiration I have given the dearly departed for years, I still feel that we shall never make a Mozart or a Haydn of him in instrumental and church composition, whereas in song he is unsurpassed . . . I think, therefore, that Schubert should be treated as a song composer by his biographers." For years to come, the "Prince of Song" was treated exactly that way, until larger instrumental works finally came to light. Spaun was to reconsider his position in the 1860s, once he knew more of Schubert's music: "While some recognition was accorded his songs in Vienna, his equally beautiful instrumental compositions were rejected . . . It is almost forty years since Schubert's death, and only now do they really know in Vienna what they possessed in him and what they lost" (SMF 30, 355).

Everyone in the 1820s was clear about the relative status of small works, no matter how brilliantly executed, in comparison with the prestigious genres. The domestic music cultivated (and sometimes composed) by dilettantes, women, and amateurs could barely hope to compete with higher forms. Schubert never abandoned these more intimate genres – indeed, part of his achievement was to raise their stature – yet he also held aspirations for large-scale works. One of the first reviews that Schubert received noted, "The young composer has tried his hand at a higher genre for the first time [a Singspiel]; it is only fair to do full justice to his praiseworthy endeavor to remain original and one day to attain to a significant rank in art" (SDB 146). That is indeed what he aimed for. In a famous letter written not long before his death, Schubert mentions "three operas, a Mass, and a symphony" so as to acquaint the publisher Schott with his "strivings after the highest in art" (SDB 740). Friends likewise refer to Schubert's "larger efforts" and the "highest branches of art" when discussing his big pieces. By the end of Schubert's lifetime, critics were sounding a similar theme. The *Wiener Zeitschrift für Kunst, Literatur, Theater und Mode* noted: "The great talent of the renowned song and romance composer is many-sided and tries itself in every branch, as do all those who possess the spirit of true and striving art" (SDB 781).

To understand the course of Schubert's professional career, therefore, we must observe how he attempted to negotiate a Viennese musical culture dominated artistically by Beethoven, theatrically by Italian operas (especially Rossini's), and commercially by "wretched fashionable stuff" (as Schubert once called it [SDB 375]). We must explore Schubert's budding fame, his dealings with the city's musical establishment, and the critical evaluation his music received, and we must speculate on the career strategy that he charted for himself.

At this point, the myth of Schubert's putative neglect intersects with another myth: that he was a "natural" composer who created so spontaneously that he had little control over what poured out of his head and onto paper. Vogl seems to be the one most responsible for this image, especially as he endlessly repeated anecdotes about Schubert's not recognizing his own songs. The distilled version is that Schubert dashed off a song at Vogl's house and left it there. As the key was not convenient, Vogl had it transposed. When Schubert later saw the recopied song on Vogl's piano, he said, "That's not bad, who is it by?" (SMF 217; cf. 101, 146, 226, 296, 362). Of course, there is a chance Vogl simply misunderstood an ironic comment: when he transposed or embellished a song, as he often did, it was no longer Schubert's.

Other friends also talk about Schubert's "natural" talent; some even link his gifts to "mesmerism" and "clairvoyance," creation accomplished in a trance-like state. Frequent comments surface about how quickly Schubert composed. Small genres work best for such flashes of inspiration: one can image a song written on a scrap of paper, but not a symphony. As a consequence of such views – combined with accounts of insufficient training in musical theory – Schubert appears to have been a great composer despite himself. Although we know that he did compose pieces rapidly, many had a longer genesis. We possess copious sketches and drafts for large compositions as well as for some songs; probably even more have disappeared and still comparatively little is known about Schubert's working methods. Moreover, Schubert carefully planned many compositions and on occasion even incorporated astounding technical features such as palindromes and mirror passages.[1]

If Schubert is represented as detached from the marvels he produced, no one would really expect him to have had much concern with their fate after creation. And in fact, during Schubert's early years friends assumed his business negotiating for him. The ultimate result of the sentimental image of a shy, poorly trained, natural genius who just wrote what he wanted, without any other motives, is that the course of Schubert's career is made to appear haphazard, unpremeditated and, except perhaps for his last works, chronologically indistinguishable. Yet if we empower Schubert by returning some conscious control over his oeuvre, then a calculated strategy begins to come into focus. We discern Schubert's struggle in the early 1820s to make his mark and to win his place in a competitive musical world. He continued to write incomparable songs, his mastery secure. Dances, part-songs, and smaller keyboard works – widely performed and published – further enhanced his growing status as a "popular" composer. He covered his bases as well with flashy virtuoso works and with liturgical pieces that were widely used in various churches and were sometimes published. At the same time, Schubert's attention increasingly turned elsewhere, first to the Rossinian world of the theater and, somewhat later, to Beethoven's domain of instrumental music.

No longer living at home, no longer teaching, and no longer earning any kind of fixed income, Schubert was now a professional composer without a permanent position or salary. He wrote his new, ambitious works for public presentation, rather than for his earlier outlets of private readings with family, at the Seminary, or with private orchestras. The events of 1820 in particular, as Leopold von Sonnleithner recognized, marked the "turning point" in Schubert's professional career. Schubert issued no bold statement, literally or symbolically, as did Haydn with the "quite new, special manner" of his Op. 33 String Quartets, as did Mozart by leaving Salzburg (and his father) and establishing himself as a freelance composer in Vienna, or as did Beethoven with the "new path" proclaimed by the *Eroica* Symphony at the start of his "heroic" middle period. Schubert's resolve was, however, just as strong, his direction just as determined, but less loudly announced.

Recognizing this direction and determination has been obscured not only by the patronizing image of a natural composer, but also by the fact that so much of Schubert's music is grouped together without regard to the circumstances of its genesis or the degree of his compositional maturity at the time of its creation. We fail to make important distinctions. When the prestigious Leipzig *Allgemeine musikalische Zeitung* reviewed the A Minor String Quartet (D804) in 1824, it called the work a "not to be despised first-born" (SDB 333). Commentators often "correct" this statement by noting that Schubert had already written more than a dozen quartets. Yet in important ways this quartet is indeed a "first-born" – the first chamber piece Schubert allowed to be performed in public, and the first (and only) quartet published during his lifetime; the first string quartet, in other words, that he acknowledged and sought to promote.

Although Schubert's characteristic modesty complicates matters somewhat, perhaps we should take him at his word when he writes to Ferdinand in 1824 that there is "nothing" to his quartets (SDB 362). He apparently considered his first symphonies apprentice works as well. Asked around 1823 to supply a promised work for performance, Schubert responded that he had "nothing for full orchestra that [he] could send out into the world with a clear conscience" (SDB 265). Some years later he made a similar remark to a publisher when he disavowed all his early symphonies (SDB 740). We see the same keen discernment leveled on his Lieder, especially in the remarkably canny choices he made as to which of among hundreds were worth publishing. In a letter to Ferdinand, Schubert says that only three of ten songs his brother had lent to a friend "seem good"; he then proceeds to list exactly what many would agree are the three strongest (SDB 363). In short, Schubert knew the worth of his compositions and made distinctions among what he considered immature exercises; pieces that helped him learn his craft; occasional works written for family, friends, the Seminary or other venues; and fully mature compositions, which displayed his mastery. Spaun states that many early works Schubert "discarded and declared to be merely preliminary studies" (SMF 359; cf. 355). Other composers – Brahms is a notorious case – destroyed youthful pieces and anything that did not please them, as well as discarding sketches so that their working methods might remain hidden. Schubert did not go so far as to erase or hide his past, but neither did he much value it. The degree to which he planned ahead, did not think that his current work was necessarily his best, and sought continuous growth may surprise many, for it runs counter to the image of a natural genius and professional naïf.

We should not be deceived by all the charming and ingenious instrumental pieces of Schubert's student years that today are admired and loved. Schubert forgot about most of them. Imagine, indeed, if posterity knew only the pieces Schubert explicitly acknowledged and promoted – the last three quartets, two piano trios, the string quintet, six piano sonatas, the "Great" C Major Symphony, and so forth. Had Beethoven carried out the suicide he apparently contemplated around the time of the Heiligenstadt Testament (1802) – in other words, at the very age Schubert died – the quality and quantity of his compositional legacy would have hardly matched Schubert's. Schubert must have hoped the first works he actively promoted were only the beginning of a long career, one that he did not know – or was reluctant to acknowledge consciously – would be cut so short.

The dawn of the decade that would be his last marked a turning point in Schubert's personal life as well. Early in 1820 Schubert was arrested. Although details remain unclear, the chilling events surrounding a police action that involved Schubert and four friends had disturbing private and, perhaps, professional consequences; the arrest gives vivid evidence of the politically charged climate of Metternich's repressive Vienna. The direst repercussions were felt by Johann Chrysostomus Senn (1795–1857), one of Schubert's close friends since their days together at the Seminary, where, even then, his liberal views had caused trouble. Senn studied law, supported himself by tutoring the children of wealthy families, and increasingly turned to writing poetry. Remembering his youth decades later, Senn offered a revealing glimpse of the earliest days of Schubert's circle:

> The German struggles for liberation, from 1813 to 1815, had left in
> their wake a significant spiritual upheaval in Austria too. Among
> other things, there was gathered in Vienna at that time, as it were by
> instinct and not as the result of any intention, a splendid,
> companionable circle of young writers, poets, artists and cultured
> people generally, such as the Imperial City had scarcely ever seen
> hitherto and which, after it was disbanded, sowed seeds for the
> future in every direction . . . My poems too, some of which Schubert
> set to music, originated partly in this circle. (SMF 334)

Schubert's letters from Zseliz in 1818 were addressed collectively to Schober, Spaun, Mayrhofer, and Senn – perhaps the best indication of who mattered most to him at the time. Some eighteen months later, however, the camaraderie was abruptly shattered. Franz von Bruchmann alluded to the fateful evening years later: "After a wildly spent night, during which we gave ourselves up to joy without a care and had no inkling of the impending disaster, you [Senn] were torn from our midst in the early morning, never to return" (SDB 130). A story later circulated that an informant had been discovered among the group, asked to leave, and, when he refused, promptly expelled; this led to the detention in the early hours of the morning. Whatever the cause, at a time of considerable distrust and political tension, gatherings of students were typically viewed with suspicion. Student societies (Burschenschaften) were officially outlawed by the Karlsbad Degrees, which followed the assassination in 1819 of the prominent playwright and royalist August von Kotzebue by a student.

The official report in March to the notorious Chief of the Secret Police, Count Josef Sedlnitzky, details what was deemed the "stubborn and insulting behavior evinced by Johann Senn, native of Pfunds in the Tyrol." Senn was not shy in telling the authorities exactly what he thought, stating that he "was not concerned at all about the police," and that "the government was too stupid to be able to penetrate his secrets." The report further claims that "Schubert, the school assistant from the Rossau," as well as Johann Zechenter and the law students Josef von Streinsberg and Bruchmann, "chimed in against the authorized official in the same tone, inveighing against him with insulting and opprobrious language." Senn would come to trial, while the other four participants would "be summoned and severely reprimanded." The police decided that Streinsberg's and Bruchmann's fathers should be "informed of their sons' conduct" (SDB 128–29).

Although Schubert appears to have been let off without punishment, he had been implicated nonetheless in a very serious matter. (Even his handwriting changed markedly around this time.) Perhaps some higher protection or his growing reputation as a composer saved him, but the incident meant that he would now have a police record, something that could cause grave problems in a bureaucratic system requiring police permission for nearly everything – employment, marriage, travel, publication, and so forth. For Senn, the consequences were devastating. After being held for fourteen months, he was expelled permanently from Vienna. He never saw Schubert again, a promising career was dashed, and nearly forty years in exile proved ruinous for him.

Senn was not forgotten; indeed, his memory haunted the circle. Bruchmann, who may have felt some guilt that his life was not likewise affected, maintained a supportive correspondence. He found Senn as passionate and committed as ever when they met in Innsbruck in 1822. He probably returned from that trip with the two Senn poems Schubert set shortly thereafter, *Selige Welt* and *Schwanengesang* (D744). Moritz von Schwind, who would soon emerge as one of Schubert's dearest friends, only met Senn years later, after Schubert's death. Well before that meeting, he wrote to Schober, "I wish with all my heart that I could know Senn."[2] There are frequent references to Senn in letters; his health was often toasted, and he apparently came to symbolize a moral compass in the face of compromise of ideals: if "Senn suddenly appeared in our midst, we should be truly ashamed of such company [the vapid new members of the reading circle]," Schwind informed Schober in 1823 (SDB 302).

When the arrest occurred, Schubert was still sharing Mayrhofer's housing in the inner city. Spaun thought that "their years living together reacted most favorably on both of them, on the poet as well as the composer." Schubert continued to set many of his friend's poems and worked on an opera, *Adrast*, to his libretto. We do not know exactly what caused the rupture between them after more than two years, perhaps aesthetic disputes, Mayrhofer's authoritarian ways, or conflicts over more personal matters. Anton Holzapfel indicates that Mayrhofer's "periods of melancholy and depression" possibly caused problems in "their day-to-day relations, perhaps on small differences of opinion regarding money matters, in which Schubert may well have been to blame." Mayrhofer himself was fairly candid in his 1829 reminiscence of Schubert: "While we lived together our idiosyncrasies could not but show themselves, we were both richly endowed in that respect, and the circumstances could not fail to appear" (SMF 21, 63, 14).

At the end of 1820, Schubert moved just a few houses away to live alone for the first time in his life. Like Beethoven, Schubert resided in many different places in Vienna.[3] Although alone during three stretches in the 1820s, this first time for more than a year, he usually shared modest rooms with friends. Perhaps it was just coincidence, perhaps advisable caution in the wake of his arrest, but for whatever reason the constituency of Schubert's core circle of friends changed gradually around the turn of the decade. The Senn incident, Spaun's transfer to the customs office in Linz, the falling out with Mayrhofer, and the dissolution of the Unsinnsgesellschaft – all these events distanced Schubert from some of his closest friends.

New figures, however, entered his life. In general, those Schubert had known from Seminary days, his somewhat older and more socially prominent friends, either left Vienna (not always by choice) or married and settled down to conventional lives. Holzapfel's 1858 account of his later contact with Schubert is typical: "Our meetings became fewer and fewer after 1818, when I began my career as a borough official. The things we had in common grew noticeably less and [Schubert] attached himself to a circle of friends quite unknown to me" (SMF 61; cf. SDB 211). And Bauernfeld recalls that Schubert "often expressed regret, in letters as well as conversation, that the friendly union of so many worthy young men, as will happen, became disrupted by their pursuing different careers and by other chances" (SMF 32). It was not only that some former friends were no longer as available to socialize, and that practical circumstances thus precluded the long tavern nights of talking and drinking Schubert so enjoyed. As Holzapfel's situation suggests, interests, viewpoints, and values often diverged as well. The free-thinking, liberal, artistic sensibility Schubert prized most highly mutated in some to a dreaded conformity. In an 1823 letter to Schober, Schubert lamented losing Bruchmann, who "seems to bend to the formalities of the world" (SDB 300). Another friend complained the following year that "many [of the circle] are abroad, many have buried themselves in pandects and codes" (SDB 342). And Bauernfeld, when he finally began his first permanent job, wrote in his diary, "It seems to me as if I were about to be hanged."[4] Among the core members of the later Schubert circle, one often senses a horror of desk jobs, marriage, and other ingredients of conventional adult life.

Despite Schober's usually being on the scene (although he, too, left Vienna for two years in August 1823), Schubert's social sphere now began to include younger friends, putting him in the position of minor celebrity and mentor rather than of apprentice and protégé. We do not know exactly when Schubert first met Leopold Kupelwieser, who was just a few months his senior; perhaps it was as early as 1813, when Kupelwieser was studying art at the same school as Schubert's brother Karl. Both Kupelwieser and Schubert were members of the Unsinnsgesellschaft and guests at Atzenbrugg Castle (managed by a relative of Schober's) in 1820 and 1821, during happy summer excursions Kupelwieser memorably captured in two famous watercolors. (One depicts the journey there in an open carriage, the other the Schubertians playing a game of charades [see page 71].) Schwind, seven years younger than Schubert, assumed special importance, especially when Spaun, Schober, and Kupelwieser were all abroad at the same time. And later in the 1820s, Schwind introduced Schubert to the dramatist Bauernfeld, who was five years younger.

Spaun, whose transfer to Linz in September 1821 meant he was the first to leave, inquired some months later as to what the "poetic-musical-painting triumvirate" of Schober, Schubert, and Kupelwieser had produced in the meantime (SDB 212). In Schubert's case, the answer was primarily operas and Singspiele. The theater offered the most customary, feasible, and attractive avenue to fame and financial reward, and it is hardly surprising that Schubert, not himself a virtuoso performer capable of promoting his own music, devoted the next several years to writing music for the stage and trying to establish some formal relationship with an opera house.

Vienna was a city captivated by all manner of spectacles – drama, ballet, and operas above all, as well as exotic animals, circuses, and natural delights encountered in the Prater, the city's largest public

8 "The Fall of Man: Schubertian Parlor Game in Atzenbrugg." This watercolor by
Leopold Kupelwieser from 1821 shows Franz von Schober as the serpent,
Kupelwieser as the tree of knowledge, and Johann Baptist Jenger as Adam.
Schubert is seated at the piano and across the room is Josef von Spaun.

park. Dramas by Shakespeare, Schiller, Lessing, and Kotzebue, serious fare delivered in high German rather than Viennese dialect, ruled
at the Burg-Theater, one of the two Imperial Court Theaters in the
inner city. The other, the so-called Kärntnertor-Theater, presented
mainly opera and ballet, and was located near the site of the current
State Opera. In addition, private suburban theaters catered to a variety
of audiences with all manner of plays, ballet, and musical theater. The
largest was the Theater an der Wien, established in 1801 by Emanual
Schikaneder, who had written the libretto for Mozart's *Magic Flute* and
created the role of Papageno. Beethoven's *Fidelio* was premiered there
in 1805, and there Schubert saw its final version in 1814. Two other
houses, the Leopoldstädter-Theater and Josefstädter-Theater, offered
more popular works, with or without music, and later nurtured the
uniquely Viennese satirical talents of Johann Nestroy and Ferdinand
Raimund, both acquaintances of Schubert.

Schubert had for many years enthusiastically attended dramatic and musical productions at the court and suburban theaters by the time he himself entered the fray in 1820.[5] As a teenager, he had composed operas and Singspiele of varying length and complexity, and, while none was publicly performed, the modest scope of some must have made domestic readings possible. As with his early symphonies, Schubert had sought in these student works to gain compositional experience and willingly did so without the prospect, or even the intention, of realizing staged performances. (In 1822, Josef Hüttenbrenner apparently tried to interest theaters in *Des Teufels Lustschloss*, Schubert's first completed opera, written eight years earlier [SDB 238].)

Schubert was composing "at Vogl's instigation, and therefore not without purpose, operas, Singspiele for performance," we learn from a letter of Anton Holzapfel in May 1819 (SDB 120). As an esteemed member of the Imperial Court Opera, one with clout and connections, Vogl was particularly well positioned to help promote Schubert's works. The friendship between the young composer and the prominent singer had deepened since their introduction in 1817, and perhaps especially during their summer excursion in 1819 to Vogl's native Steyr and to Linz. The work alluded to in the letter quoted above was *Die Zwillingsbrüder* (The Twin Brothers), to a text by Georg von Hofmann, in which Vogl would perform the parts of the twin brothers Franz and Friedrich. Schubert composed the one-act Singspiel, the music of which lasts under an hour, in January 1819. It premiered in June 1820 at the Kärntnertor-Theater. Six performances over the next five weeks met with mixed reviews: "The general verdict can only be favorable, although not to the point to which [Schubert's] numerous friends endeavor to force it" (SDB 138–39). The work was reviewed even in Dresden and Leipzig periodicals, the former critic warning of "excess" (a word that appears frequently in later reviews of many of Schubert's works) and stating: "The public acclaimed the operetta like a great masterpiece, which it is not" (SDB 139). The longest review appeared in Vienna's *Allgemeine musikalische Zeitung*. Aware that this was Schubert's first major notice, the sympathetic critic felt bound "to weigh each word and to do no injury to the tender blossom." Sensitive that Schubert was Viennese, that this was "homegrown art," the thoughtful criticism is remarkably consistent with later comments about Schubert's theater music generally. The end of the opera "gave occasion for party strife, Schubert's friends wishing to call him and a great many serpents hissing their dissent" (SDB 135–38).

Schubert's relatively successful debut as a stage composer was bolstered just a few weeks later with eight performances of Die Zauberharfe (The Magic Harp), a three-act magical melodrama commissioned by the Theater an der Wien. (Schubert eventually published its overture as part of Rosamunde, a later theater piece.) Bauernfeld, who did not yet know Schubert, characterized the music as "excellent" in his diary. Reviews strike a note similar to those of Die Zwillingsbrüder, praising Schubert's score for its originality and beauty, which "once again proves his talent" (SDB 149). The critical reactions to both pieces make clear that theater music essentially marked Schubert's debut as a public composer, that his first stage works were fairly popular and generally well received, that association with Vienna's active theatrical life could bring considerable attention even in the foreign press, and finally that Schubert's friends played a role in the success of these pieces, just as they did in promoting his other music. One Viennese critic predicted that Schubert "will do great and beautiful things, and it is in this hope that we welcome the modest artist very cordially" (SDB 139). For a twenty-three-year-old composer, one whose name had rarely as yet been mentioned in any periodical, to find his work cheered nightly by the public and then discussed in important journals must have been a heady experience.

Following all this prominent attention elicited by the stage works during the summer of 1820, the new musical season began that would change Schubert's stature and set the pattern for his relation to various types of audiences. In Vienna at the time there were three interrelated domains of musical activity – private, semi-public, and public – comprising a diverse mixture of listeners and performers. The differences among them were based less on the social class of the participants than on repertory, taste, and venue; Schubert was deeply involved in all of these spheres. Although Vienna had several small spaces that were used for public concerts, much music-making took place at home; this was true not only for the "intimate" Schubert, but even for the "public" Beethoven and Rossini. Beethoven's large instrumental works and Rossini's operas were endlessly domesticated, arranged for keyboard and for almost every conceivable instrumental combination negotiable by amateur musicians. Beethoven himself arranged his Second Symphony and Septet for piano trio. The musical culture of the time was saturated with arrangements, and publishers' catalogues were crammed with reworkings for popular domestic instruments (especially piano, flute, and guitar) rather than with symphonies or serious string quartets, which usually required larger and more professional ensembles and which sold less well.

The principal reason we associate Schubert's music with such intimate gatherings is that they had a name: Schubertiades, unpublicized events devoted primarily or exclusively to his music. Usually given by the composer's more well-to-do friends and patrons (although not the high-ranking men that supported Beethoven), they offered an informal, sociable atmosphere that often included recitations, eating, drinking, and dancing. The number of participants at a Schubertiade could range from a handful to over a hundred, and their frequency varied; some years saw weekly gatherings (or more), other years saw none. We know of some Schubertiades held in other cities when Schubert would visit, some were held in his absence and after his death. (Bauernfeld recalled that "many a Schubertiade had to take place without Schubert, if he did not happen to be in a sociable mood or if one or another guest was not particularly congenial to him" [SMF 229].) Kupelwieser, away in Rome in 1824, describes what would appear to be a "solo" Schubertiade ("I treat myself to a Schubertiade now and again"), which suggests that what was really needed was just an instrument, some compositions, and a desire to immerse oneself in Schubert's music (SDB 332). Schubertiades were certainly events but also, perhaps, a state of mind, and for that reason they continue to this day in the form of numerous Schubert concerts and festivals worldwide.

Schubertiades enraptured Schubert's closest friends, as well as more distant acquaintances. No written programs were provided, and only occasionally does a letter or diary mention the specific compositions heard on a given evening. Schubert performed often, usually accompanying singers such as Vogl, Baron Karl Schönstein, Sophie Müller, and Josefine Fröhlich; sometimes he sang or improvised. Lieder predominated, together with dances, partsongs, and keyboard works, especially for four hands. Missing, for the most part, were the piano sonatas and chamber music, though occasionally they too appeared.

One does not deprecate Schubert's social music by observing that he sought to entertain and to communicate directly with his listeners. Indeed, a distinctive trait of Schubert's artistic achievement is that despite the brevity and intimacy of a Lied or piano miniature, which may point toward the trivial, in his hands such small-scale pieces often acquire extraordinary depth and significance. Nor should we underestimate the satisfaction that these forums gave Schubert, especially early in his career. Every composer desires an audience, and Schubert initially found passionate, enthusiastic, and devoted listeners in the people he cared about most – his family and friends. This artistic confirmation may, in fact, have lessened his need to give public concerts.

The atmosphere of the Schubertiade spilled over into somewhat more formal semi-public (or semi-private) concerts, such as musical evenings held at the home of Ignaz Sonnleithner about twice a month during the musical season from 1815 to 1824. Amateurs and professionals alike performed before a select audience that could number a hundred or more. Arranged and directed by Ignaz's son, and Schubert's friend, Leopold, the cantata *Prometheus* was performed to great acclaim in January 1819. The vocal quartet *Das Dörfchen* enjoyed equal praise later that year. More important was a performance of

Erlkönig by August Ritter von Gymnich and pianist Anna Fröhlich on 1 December 1820 (SMF 342–43). Such salons were an important forum for Schubert, and, although again we seldom know what exactly was played, the premieres of many works, even of symphonies, took place at these sorts of gatherings.

Some of those involved with Sonnleithner's musical salons had already helped to found the Gesellschaft der Musikfreunde (Society of the Friends of Music) in 1812. Schubert's relationship with this famous organization remains somewhat mysterious. As early as 1818, his name appeared on a poster initiating a series of concerts of vocal and chamber music called Musikalische Abendunterhaltungen (Musical Evening Entertainments). Evidently, the initial plan was to perform his works in the illustrious company of those by Haydn, Mozart, Beethoven, and others, but for some unknown reason Schubert's proposed membership was denied. When he did join in March 1822, he quickly assumed higher official positions. The Society sponsored another series as well, the Gesellschaftskonzerte (Society Concerts), which were given three or four Sundays a year in the Imperial Palace. Only three of Schubert's compositions, two part-songs and an overture, appeared in this series, all during the 1821 and 1822 seasons. Performances in January 1820 of *Der Wanderer* and *Erlkönig* – Schubert's two most popular songs during his lifetime – finally marked Schubert's debut in the Musical Evening Entertainments, which became the most prominent venue for presentations of his Lieder and vocal quartets during the 1820s. Otto Biba, the archivist of the Society today, has discovered that Schubert's music was in fact performed more frequently in this series from 1825 until his death than any other composer's except the adored Rossini; he surpassed even Mozart and Beethoven.[6]

Finally, Schubert's music was heard at public concerts for which admission was charged. Even in the absence of a satisfactory concert hall until the 1830s or of permanently established orchestras (except for those connected with the theaters), virtuosos, composers, and charity organizations were still able to present "academies," as public concerts were usually called. Held in theaters, ballrooms (Redoutensäle), taverns, and in other large spaces, these events offered the possibility of hearing what often turned out to be a bewildering mixture of art forms, pieces, arrangements, improvisations, and genres. In contrast to the churchlike reverence observed in concert halls today, where even clapping between movements is considered a *faux pas*, audiences applauded during pieces when they liked something and indicated their desire to hear pieces repeated, which was common. One can only guess at the general level of technical execution when, for instance, a freelance orchestra would present a new symphony, often without a conductor, after only one or two rehearsals – or none!

As early as 1823 Schubert had contemplated giving a "public Schubertiade" devoted entirely to his music (SDB 314). Such events were relatively rare, required elaborate planning, and entailed considerable financial risk. Even Beethoven had fewer than a dozen academies during his entire thirty-five years in Vienna. His last, in 1824, which saw the première of the Ninth Symphony, seems to have spurred Schubert's hopes to give one himself, but nothing came of this until his final year. When Schubert's music was heard in public, therefore, it was as part of concerts given by others. The first two public performances of secular works by him – an overture and the song *Schäfers Klagelied* – occurred at the hall of the Zum römischen Kaiser (Roman Emperor), a first-class hotel in the inner city, in concerts organized in 1818 and 1819 by violinist Eduard Jaëll. Some years later Schubert's mature chamber music began to appear in smaller halls, most notably performed by the noted string quartet of the illustrious Ignaz Schuppanzigh, Beethoven's favored violinist.

Charity organizations also presented Schubert's music, as when the annual benefit concert organized by the Gesellschaft adeliger Frauen zur Beförderung des Guten und Nützlichen (Society of Ladies of the Nobility for the Promotion of the Good and the Useful) offered the public première of *Erlkönig* on 7 March 1821 in the Kärntnertor-Theater. Held on Ash Wednesday, when theaters were closed, this was

9 The Kärntnertor-Theater, where Schubert's *Die Zwillingsbrüder* premiered in
1820 and the first public performance of *Erlkönig* took place the next year.

one of the most important social events of the year. With three compositions, *Erlkönig* and two multi-voice works, *Das Dörfchen* and *Gesang der
Geister über den Wassern* (D714), Schubert dominated a program consisting also of music by Mozart, Spohr, Gyrowetz, Voříšek, Boieldieu,
Bernhard Romberg, and Rossini. The evening offered a typical mixture of Lieder and partsongs, arias and duets, overtures, concerto
movements, dancing, recitation, and tableaux. Anselm Hüttenbrenner later described the event:

> Vogl sang the song so splendidly and with such enthusiasm that
> *Erlkönig* had to be repeated. I played the accompaniment on a new
> grand piano by Konrad Graf. Schubert, who could have played his
> own compositions as well as I, was too shy to be induced to do so; he
> contented himself with standing near me and turning pages. (SMF
> 186)

Spaun never forgot the "rapt attention and general tempestuous
applause the large audience awarded both composer and singer."
Without exception, critics recognized Schubert's rare musical gifts:
"excellently sung by Vogl; [*Erlkönig*] made a great effect. A master-

piece of musical painting"; "the music shows much imagination. Several successful passages were justly acclaimed by the public"; "a composition full of fantasy and feeling"; and "We wish the young composer good luck on his first successful endeavor which has been awarded the loud applause of the public through the excellent performances by Vogl in both private circles and public academies".[7]

Some months prior to Vogl's decisive performance of Erlkönig, a rare instance in which he sang a Schubert Lied in public, the Dresden *Abendzeitung* had reported that:

> The young composer Schuberth [sic] has set to music several songs by the best poets (mostly Goethe), which testify to the profoundest studies combined with genius worthy of admiration, and attract the eyes of the cultivated musical world. He knows how to paint in sound, and the songs *Die Forelle*, *Gretchen am Spinnrade*, and *Der Kampf*, surpass in characteristic truth all that may be found in the domain of song. They are not yet published but go from hand to hand only in manuscript copies. (SDB 155)

Rectifying that situation was the logical next step in Schubert's budding career. Publication would lead to more detailed reviews and greater exposure beyond Vienna, but Schubert's modesty initially forced others to be his advocates. Five years earlier, an ambitious plan had been devised to issue eight volumes of songs to poetry by Schiller, Klopstock, Matthisson, Hölty, Salis-Seewis, and others, but this venture for some unknown reason did not materialize.

In connection with that project, Spaun wrote to Goethe in the spring of 1816 with the hope of attracting his interest, first by introducing Schubert as a nineteen-year-old composer whom "nature endowed from the tenderest childhood with the most pronounced leanings towards the art of music, gifts which Salieri, the Nestor among composers, brought to fair maturity with the most unselfish love of art. The general acclamation accorded the young artist for the present songs." By publishing his songs, Spaun tells Goethe, the "modest" composer will "doubtless shortly take his place in that rank among German composers to which his preeminent talents assign him." Then Spaun appeals more directly, offering Schubert's songs as a testimonial gift, because it was to Goethe's

> glorious poetry [that Schubert] is indebted not only for the origin of a great part of them, but also, in all essentials, for his development into a German songwriter. Himself too modest, however, to regard his works as worthy of the great honor of bearing a name so highly celebrated throughout the reach of the German tongue, he lacks the courage to request so great a favor of Your Excellency in person, and I, one of his friends, saturated as I am by his melodies, thus venture to ask Your Excellency in his name. (SDB 56–57)

This letter gives some indication of the overwhelming importance that Germany's greatest living poet exerted on Schubert's first masterpieces. Although Goethe returned the neatly copied music without comment, Schubert's champions continued their efforts. The next year they sent Erlkönig to Breitkopf & Härtel, the prestigious Leipzig publishing firm, only to meet with further indifference. (The song was in fact returned to the wrong Franz Schubert, another composer with the same name working in Dresden, who wrote an indignant letter saying he would never have composed such "trash" [SDB 76].)

A few years later, after the highly acclaimed private, semi-public, and public performances of 1820 and 1821, the time was finally right for publication, even if the project still encountered complications. Leopold von Sonnleithner recalled that "suddenly Schubert's name was talked of in all musical circles and people asked why [Erlkönig] was not published." Sonnleithner says that various publishers rejected Erlkönig because "the composer was unknown and because of the difficulty of the piano accompaniment" (SMF 108; cf. 344). Undaunted, Sonnleithner and a few other supporters themselves undertook to cover the expenses of publishing the song. It was first offered for sale at one of the private musical salons at his father's house, where guests immediately snatched up all the copies.

There is a striking disparity between the trouble Schubert encountered getting any song published and the unusual success his first publications actually enjoyed. Stories about Schubert's frustrating relations with publishers have been repeated so often, and accepted so uncritically, that they have come to exemplify his troubled professional circumstances in general. (For some commentators, it seems, bad news is good news, necessary, in fact, to promote the legend of Schubert's neglect.) The reluctance to release *Erlkönig* seems curious for a piece as famous as chroniclers and critics reported and as initial sales confirmed. One would think that astute publishers such as Anton Diabelli and Tobias Haslinger would have appreciated the merits of Schubert's Lieder – here were pieces that could make some money. The quantity of printings and reprintings was exceptionally large, and both publishers, even if initially cautious, later reaped considerable financial gain from Schubert's compositions.

Whatever reservations Diabelli may have had about Schubert's Lieder soon evaporated. In Spaun's words, "the spell was broken and publishers gradually accepted his compositions" (SMF 134). Again, in the effort to portray Schubert as grossly underrated and neglected, commentators have overlooked the fact that Diabelli made his own guitar arrangements of the accompaniments, usually releasing them around the same time as the piano originals. In addition, Diabelli soon published Anselm Hüttenbrenner's *Erlkönig Walzer*, an affectionate popularization of the song. In rapid succession, the firm of Cappi & Diabelli issued other volumes of Lieder on commission, many of them alternatively available with guitar accompaniment. The selection and grouping of works, as well as the choice of their dedications, show what adept decisions Schubert and his friends made from among the hundreds of songs available when determining which should be presented to the public. In 1821 and 1822, there were eleven releases (Opp. 1–8 and 12–14) containing a total of thirty-two songs. Whereas *Erlkönig* and *Gretchen am Spinnrade* were given individual opus numbers, 1 and 2 respectively, all the others were in collections of two, three, four, or five songs; among the best known are *Heidenröslein*, *Der Wanderer*, *Rastlose*

Liebe, and *Nähe des Geliebten*. Throughout his remaining six years Schubert was well paid for his songs; he could earn the equivalent of the annual salary of a minor civil servant from a dozen of them.

The only nonvocal work to appear in 1821 was Op. 9, a collection of thirty-six waltzes in two books; it included another of Schubert's most popular and widely known pieces – the "Trauerwalzer" ("Mourning Waltz" – a nick-name Schubert allegedly thought ridiculous – "Who would write a mourning waltz?" he asked). Three charming partsongs for two tenors and two basses were released as Op. 11, the sort of Biedermeier barbershop harmony that enchanted audiences of the day and that has enjoyed a revival in recent years. The stream of songs, dances, partsongs, and keyboard music continued for the rest of Schubert's life and constituted the vast majority of his published oeuvre. We do not know much about how Schubert made some of his career decisions or with whom he consulted. On the one hand, Sonnleithner, Josef Hüttenbrenner, and others who initially played such prominent roles negotiating with publishers and impresarios were not among Schubert's intimate circle. On the other hand, his working partnerships with much closer friends, such as Mayrhofer and Schober, led to the active creation of compositions. In any case, Schubert himself eventually began to take a more active role in charting and promoting his career; as he wrote to Sonnleithner, "my future fate concerns me greatly after all" (SDB 264).

An advantage of the publication of these small-scale works, which were soon followed by two larger keyboard pieces – the Eight Variations on a French Song, Op. 10 (dedicated to Beethoven) and the "Wanderer" Fantasy, Op. 15 – was increased chances for Schubert's music to be heard beyond Vienna and to attract serious critical evaluation. The many reviews of his two theater works and of the Ash Wednesday concert in 1821 generally did not offer the depth of insight that might have come from more reasoned criticism prompted by publication, such as two long and enthusiastic reviews from 1822. They were the only comprehensive Viennese surveys of Schubert's music during his lifetime, and they give some insights into contemporaneous views of the Lied and of Schubert's achievements with these "masterpieces" (SDB 206–08, 214–18).

While the public was beginning to catch up with some of his older compositions, Schubert was trying to move forward with new and more ambitious projects, reaching toward those "higher" genres he hoped might elevate his reputation. Well-positioned supporters at the Court Opera continued to help. Vogl had already arranged the performances of *Die Zwillingsbrüder* and probably suggested to the Kärntnertor-Theater that it commission Schubert to provide an aria and duet (D723) to be inserted into Ferdinand Hérold's *Das Zauberglöckchen* (The Magic Bell). According to Spaun, neither the public nor his friends knew of Schubert's involvement, yet exactly these two numbers were the best received: "This success was all the more to Schubert's credit as he did not owe it to any patronage, and as even that active group that said Schubert had no talent writing for the stage, also took part in it" (SMF 24).

In February 1821, Count Moritz Dietrichstein, a high Imperial Court official and an able composer himself, who had long taken an interest in Schubert's career, became the director of the Court Theaters. He had written a glowing testimonial just a month earlier in support of Schubert's applications for a job as composer, coach, or conductor at the opera; Schubert may even have held one of these positions for a short time. Schubert's dedication of *Erlkönig* to Dietrichstein pleased him enormously; as he remarked in a letter to Vogl, "Ever since I fathomed the genius of this young, vigorous, extraordinarily promising composer, it is among my dearest wishes to work for him *sub umbra alarum tuarum*, in so far as it is in my power" (SDB 161–62).

Two new large theater projects dwarfed all earlier efforts. Enlisting Schober as librettist, Schubert began writing *Alfonso und Estrella*, a Romantic through-composed opera in three acts, which tells a somewhat incoherent story on a medieval theme of young lovers who triumph over various political and personal intrigues. The friends began working intensively while traveling together in September 1821, a scene Schober described in a letter to Spaun:

Our room at St Pölten was particularly snug: the twin beds, a sofa
next to the warm stove, and a piano made it all very domestic and
cozy. In the evenings we always compared notes on what we had
done during the day, then sent for beer, smoked our pipe and read,
or else Sophie and Nettel came over and there was singing. (SDB
195)

Building on earlier successes, and banking on the support of sympathetic administrators, Schubert and Schober had good reason to be
optimistic. As Spaun recalled in 1829, "Everything now justified the
hope that, under the protection of the directors of the Court Opera,
Schubert would find an opportunity for getting his operas performed"
(SMF 24). Word of Schubert's projects was even spreading beyond
Vienna. A Dresden paper reported in July 1821 that "the excellent
song-writer Schubert is said to be occupied at present with the composition of a grand romantic opera" (SDB 175).

When a German opera appeared the next season, however, it was
not by Schubert. Carl Maria von Weber's *Der Freischütz* proved a considerable success when it opened in November, and no one was more
impressed than Schubert, who must also have been encouraged that a
German work could do so well. Weber came to Vienna in mid-
February 1822 to conduct some performances, and Spaun relates that
"Schubert was at Weber's almost every day and they had become very
close friends" (SMF 137). By the end of the month, Schubert had completed *Alfonso und Estrella*. Suddenly, however, the Viennese operatic
situation changed drastically. Spaun, who had been so optimistic
regarding Schubert's chances, recalled that

unfortunately hope was frustrated when the administration of the
Court Opera came to an end in 1821 and the opera house was leased to
[the Italian Impresario Domenico] Barbaja. The best members of the
German Opera Company were lost to it; even the irreplaceable Vogl
was retired and the very mediocre German company that remained
found it impossible to arouse the same interest as the extremely
brilliant Italian company. (SMF 24)

Barbaja, who concurrently ran the main opera houses in Venice and Naples, took control of both the Kärntnertor-Theater and the Theater an der Wien and scored his first coup by arranging a visit from Europe's most popular living composer. Rossini arrived in March 1822 for a three-month stay, and the tide turned irrevocably toward Italian opera. Rossini's music had first captivated Vienna in 1816, when L'inganno felice was performed at the Kärntnertor-Theater. What was not to love about these inspired, innovative, and delightful operas? No matter the ensuing setbacks to his own career, Schubert genuinely admired Rossini. Some years earlier he had written two overtures "in the Italian Style" [D590; D591], which is to say, à la Rossini, and the same influence is to be found in early symphonies, instrumental works, and even in a few Lieder.

When Schubert wrote to Spaun late in 1822, sending the Op. 13 Lieder dedicated to him, he assessed the frustrating situation in this way:

> With the opera [Alfonso und Estrella] I did not get on in Vienna. I asked to have it back and it came. Vogl has really left the theater, too. I shall shortly send it either to Dresden, whence I had a very promising letter from Weber, or to Berlin . . . With me things would be fairly well, if only the miserable business with the opera were not so galling. (SDB 248)

And so, although discouraged, Schubert was not defeated. If performances of his operas were not possible in Vienna's current climate, he would look elsewhere and enlist the help of powerful musicians (rather than administrators) such as Weber and the famous singers Wilhelmine Schröder-Devrient and Anna Milder.

Hopes for advancement through opera consumed much of Schubert's time, energy, and emotional resources in the early 1820s, even as he continued to write, although less prolifically, the "popular" pieces that sold so well and won such acclaim in frequent performances. At the same time, Schubert experienced protracted difficulties

composing certain kinds of works, a situation that has led some
scholars to call 1818–23 his "years of crisis."[8] Simply put, for extended
periods Schubert shunned genres that had deeply engaged him earlier
and in which he would later create some of his finest compositions.
Between 1810 and 1816, for instance, he composed at least thirteen
string quartets, but did not finish another one until 1824. "Finish" is
the key word, for in 1820 Schubert started a wonderful Quartet in C
Minor (D703), but stopped after the opening of the second movement.

Remarkably, however, many of Schubert's torsos from these years
are among his masterpieces; they often point to the future, not only of
his own compositional path, but of Romantic music more generally.
Pre-eminent among these works is the Symphony in B Minor (D759),
the "Unfinished," although its two movements (plus an incomplete
third) are in fact among many other movements of unfinished symphonies by Schubert that survive. Some of them are quite preliminary
(such as D615 and D708a), but that has not stopped musicologists and
composers from producing performing versions. The sketches for a
Symphony in D (D708a) in particular reveal Schubert going well
beyond the classical models of his six earlier completed symphonies.[9]

The Symphony in E Major (D729), which Schubert worked on in the
summer of 1821, reached a far more advanced state. He drafted all four
movements to the extent that the melodies, formal structure, and
basic harmonic scheme are clear. He even indicated some of the
instrumentation and fully orchestrated the first 110 measures of the
opening movement. In 1845, Ferdinand Schubert gave this torso to
Felix Mendelssohn as a gift. In a touching letter of thanks,
Mendelssohn states: "It seems to me as though, through the very
incompleteness of the work, through the scattered, half-finished
indications, I got to know your brother personally, and more closely
and more intimately than I could have done through a completed
piece. It is as though I saw him there working in his room" (SMF 414).
We will never know why Schubert abandoned this symphony – perhaps the immediate prospects for *Alfonso* made him concentrate on

that work – but orchestrations by John F. Barnett, Felix Weingartner, Brian Newbould, and others give an excellent idea of the flavor and scope of this aspiring symphony.

The fame and brilliance of the "Unfinished" Symphony justify a more detailed discussion of its origins and unusual destiny, as well as of its aborted state. Schubert wrote out a neat, fully orchestrated score of the first two movements, which he dated "Vienna, 30 October 1822." The Allegro moderato and Andante con moto herald a new Romantic sound in their use of the orchestra, provide an unparalleled example of Schubert's lyrical instrumental writing, show yet again his harmonic daring, and project a haunting quality that conveys a new range of emotions. On the reverse side of the final page of the second movement he begins a scherzo in full orchestral score, but after nine measures the manuscript ends. Was the rest of the symphony lost, or did Schubert choose not to complete the work for some unknown reason? Whatever the case, sketches and score fragments of a third movement disprove the idea that Schubert initially intended only a two-movement work, perhaps along the lines of Beethoven's two-movement piano sonatas.

The evidence strongly suggests that Schubert did not finish the piece. For one thing, there are detailed drafts for the first two movements, only incomplete ones for the third, and none at all for a final one. (Some have suggested that the "Entr'acte" in B Minor of *Rosamunde*, written around the same time and using the same orchestration and key, might have originally been the final movement.) Moreover, a couple of decades ago the next orchestrated page of the third movement was discovered – in other words, the second page of the scherzo – and it shows that Schubert did indeed break off composing after about forty measures. The question remains: why is this glorious work unfinished? Answers range from fictitious ones posed in movies (that Schubert died while writing it) to more sensible speculations (that once he lost the thread of inspiration it usually could not be reclaimed). There are suggestions that perhaps Schubert was displeased with the third movement (the surviving section of the scherzo does seem rather ordinary) and felt he could not match the innovations and magnificence of what preceded. The issue will probably never be definitively resolved; it may simply be that this exceptional work held painful associations – for, as we shall see, exactly at the time of its composition Schubert contracted the disease that changed the course of his life.

The fate of the symphony was also extraordinary. Schubert gave the score to his friend Josef Hüttenbrenner so that his brother Anselm might deliver it to the Styrian Musical Society in gratitude for its bestowing honorary membership on him. Musicologist Maynard Solomon has noted that symphonies were rarely performed there in their entirety and that sending an "unfinished" work to Graz in no way precluded one or both movements from being presented.[10] If Schubert therefore did not quite banish the work to oblivion, he did not return to complete it either. So far as we know, he never again mentioned the symphony and it languished in Anselm Hüttenbrenner's Graz home for more than forty years. In the 1860s, the prominent Viennese conductor Johann Herbeck learned of its existence and diplomatically secured the work from Anselm for performance (the diplomacy involved performing an overture by Hüttenbrenner on the same program). The belated première in 1865 astonished and delighted Viennese audiences and critics.

Other unfinished pieces establish that not only symphonies caused Schubert problems as he pursued innovative compositional paths. In February 1820, he began an oratorio, Lazarus, oder: Die Feier der Auferstehung (D689), but completed only the first and most of the second of its three acts. The text is by the theologian August Hermann Niemeyer, who believed in conveying the sentiments of a religious story rather than in operatic presentations of characters and situations. Schubert experimented with techniques he would develop further in Alfonso und Estrella, mixing recitatives and more lyrical sections in a manner that occasionally approaches Wagnerian through-composition. Lazarus may have been derailed by his arrest in the Senn incident, and when Schubert got "off track" with a piece he rarely picked up the thread again. (A notable exception is the Mass in A-flat, begun in November 1819, to which Schubert returned in 1822, and further revised four years later.) A number of opera projects during this time, including *Adrast* and *Sakuntala*, were abandoned as well.

The so-called *Quartettsatz*, the C minor work mentioned earlier, is the unfinished chamber masterpiece from this time. Schubert composed the extraordinary first movement late in 1820, but set aside the piece after some forty measures into the second movement. A thoroughly professional work, this composition points the way to Schubert's mature quartets, and leaves behind the easier charm of earlier ones written for family consumption. As he had with the unfinished symphonies, *Lazarus*, and the incomplete "Reliquie" Piano Sonata in C Major (D840) from 1825, Schubert reached an impasse at some point in the compositional process that made him abandon magnificent pieces. Part of the difficulty may have been finding a convincing way to proceed after unconventional opening movements that reinterpret traditional sonata form. Indeed, the "Wanderer" Fantasy of 1822 is one of the few completed large-scale works from these years, and it is one of Schubert's most radical rethinkings in that four movements are merged into one while simultaneously projecting a sonata design.

Despite Schubert's frustrations with unperformed operas and unfinished instrumental works, the opening years of the 1820s must have provided considerable professional satisfaction. *Die Zwillingsbrüder* and *Die Zauberharfe* introduced his name; some of his songs, dances, and partsongs took Vienna by storm; and, in Vienna and elsewhere, critical response was largely favorable. As Schubert passed gradually from student to mature composer, he tried alternatively to succeed on the stage with operas and Singspiele and to find a distinctive compositional voice that could exist alongside that of the incomparable Beethoven. Producing fewer chamber works and symphonies and finding himself unable to finish much of what he started, Schubert's attempts at "higher" genres nonetheless were among the most innovative and compelling works he ever composed. Indeed, many pieces have obtained repertory status despite their lack of completion.

The struggles reflected in so much of Schubert's music at the turn of the decade antedated the devastating upheavals in his personal life that occurred a few years later. This is not to say that the music prefigured the life: Schubert's compositional "crisis" accompanied his entry into full artistic maturity and is perhaps better viewed as growth pains than as existential pain. We shall now examine in greater depth Schubert's art and life as he commenced a new stage. The personal, creative, and professional dualisms that were integral to his psychological make-up, that find such candid expression in his music, and that he negotiated with only limited success in his career, took an unexpected and tragic turn late in 1822 and profoundly changed the remaining six years of his life. The health Schubert valued and the grave illness he endured ultimately became a struggle between life and death. As in so many of the works Schubert would compose during his remaining years, a disturbing violence interrupted the lyricism of his life.

5 Dark Schubert: "A black-winged demon of sorrow and melancholy"

> There were also times when a black-winged demon of sorrow and melancholy forced its way into [Schubert's] vicinity – not altogether an evil spirit, it is true, since, in the dark, consecrated hours, it often brought out songs of the most agonizing beauty.
>
> Eduard von Bauernfeld, 1869 (SMF 234)

Schubert had been seriously ill for more than a year when he penned unusually anguished words to Leopold Kupelwieser on the last day of March 1824:

> In a word, I feel myself the most unhappy and wretched creature in the world. Imagine a man whose health will never be right again, and who in sheer despair over this ever makes things worse and worse, instead of better; imagine a man, I say, whose most brilliant hopes have perished, to whom the happiness of love and friendship have nothing to offer but pain, at best, whose enthusiasm (at least of the stimulating kind) for all things beautiful threatens to disappear, and I ask you, is he not a miserable, unhappy being?

Schubert reached out desperately to his close friend, who was in Rome painting and studying art: "at last I can once again wholly pour out my soul to someone." He had confided to Schober earlier: "I hope to regain my health, and this recovered treasure will let me forget many a sorrow" (SMF 301). While the omnipresence of the sick and the dying in an overcrowded city such as Vienna made illness and mortality all-too-familiar aspects of everyday life, perhaps this familiarity also made them somewhat less terrifying. Grave illness only intensified an acquaintance with death that Schubert had known for years. His mother died when he was fifteen; only five of fourteen siblings from his father's first marriage survived childhood.

Although Schubert's health had apparently been robust until this point, letters make painfully clear that he was under no illusions once it was shattered: his life was forever changed. He first alluded to being sick in late February 1823 – "the circumstances of my health still forbid me to leave the house" – and for the next two years his condition was a prime concern in letters among friends (SDB 270). We do not know many details about the first few months of his illness. His isolation, in fact, even arose as a topic in one of Beethoven's conversation books from August 1823, when Karl Beethoven informs his uncle that "they greatly praise Schubert, but it is said that he hides himself" (SDB 288).

While the exact chronology and particulars of 1823 remain unclear (at some point, perhaps in the fall, he apparently spent some time in the hospital), we can partially chart the course of his health in surviving letters, mainly from Schubert or Schwind to Schober, who was away for two years in Breslau, and to Kupelwieser in Rome. In 1822 Schubert apparently lived at times with Schober, but with the onset of illness he moved back to his parent's house in the Rossau. (A letter to Spaun with that address dates from 7 December.) By mid summer 1823 Schubert felt well enough to travel with Vogl to Upper Austria, although he was nonetheless still in constant correspondence with his doctors. He wrote Schober, "I am fairly well. Whether I shall ever be completely healthy again I am inclined to doubt" (SDB 286).

The time Schubert spent in beautiful natural surroundings agreed with him, and in the fall he was relieved by the improved "state of [his] health, which (thank God) seems to be firmly restored at last" (SDB 300). Returning to Vienna in September, he shared a room in the inner city with Josef Huber, called "tall Huber" within the circle. At the end of 1823, Schwind observed that "Schubert is better, and it will not be long before he goes about with his own hair again, which had to be shorn owing to the rash. He wears a very cozy wig." The cozy wig was off by February, Schwind detected the "first signs of sweet curls," and he informed Schober that "Schubert now keeps a fourteen-day fast and confinement. He looks much better and is very bright, very comically hungry, and composes" (SDB 314, 327). The winter and spring of 1824 saw continued curative fluctuations, but they were also one of the most productive periods of Schubert's life. That summer he made his second trip to Zseliz, once again to teach Count Esterházy's children. Surely he would not have taken this position (nor would it have been offered), had his condition not improved significantly. By the end of his Hungarian stay, Schubert could take comfort in reporting that for five months he had been "in good health." Back in Vienna by mid October and living once again with his parents, Schubert, about two years after the onset of the illness, was by all indications rested and fairly well – at least for the time being.[1]

What caused this violent upheaval in his life? While it is impossible to offer definitive posthumous diagnoses, especially in a case where compromising materials may have been intentionally destroyed, physicians and biographers, after examining the surviving evidence, have concluded almost unanimously that Schubert contracted syphilis, possibly in late 1822. The various specific references to his symptoms and treatments – rashes, aches and pains, and so forth – are consistent with the primary and secondary stages of the disease. Schwind alludes to Schubert's "drinking of tea by the gallon," "new treatments," and "regimes." Schubert spent time socially with his doctor, J. Bernhard – there were even plans for the two to write an opera together – and he dedicated his Six grandes marches (D819) to him.

Otto Erich Deutsch first delicately broached the nature of Schubert's illness in a 1907 article, though there had been hints much earlier. While Schober never wrote his memoirs, he apparently talked to the journalist Ludwig August Frankl in the late 1860s. Frankl reports him saying that

Schubert let himself go to pieces; he frequented the outskirts of the city and roamed around in taverns, at the same time admittedly composing his most beautiful songs in them, just as he did in the hospital too (the Müllerlieder, according to Hölzel), where he found himself as the result of excessively indulgent sensual living and its consequences. (SMF 266)

A decade earlier, to assist in a biographical project then underway, Josef Kenner provided unusually candid information about Schubert and Schober. (Although after their early days together at the Seminary, Schubert had little contact with Kenner, who lived in Linz, he set three of his poems and dedicated one of them, Der Liedler, to him in 1825.) Kenner remarked on how Schubert's "body, strong as it was, succumbed to the cleavage in his – souls – as I would put it, of which one pressed heavenwards and the other bathed in slime." He made a similar observation a short time later: "Anyone who knew Schubert knows how he was made of two natures, foreign to each other, how powerfully the craving for pleasure dragged his soul down to the slough of moral degradation." Kenner thought it "indispensable for the biographer's grasp" of Schubert that he divulge this unpleasant information, especially as the illness "probably caused [Schubert's] premature death and certainly hastened it" (SMF 82, 86). Wilhelm von Chézy, son of the playwright Helmina von Chézy, who apparently did not know the composer well, wrote in his 1863 autobiography that "unfortunately Schubert, with his liking of the pleasures of life, had strayed onto those wrong paths which generally admit no return, at least no healthy one" (SMF 261).

As the Schober memories may not be reliable, as neither Kenner nor Chézy had much contact with Schubert in the 1820s, and as these opinions all came decades after the fact, it would not be unreasonable to discount such testimony were there not various other insinuations that link Schubert's dissipated ways to his illness. Already during his lifetime, remarks were made about behavior that must be considered dangerous and even self-destructive, especially once his constitution was damaged by syphilis. Friends report Schubert's being "well behaved" and so forth, which further suggests that there are aspects of his life and conduct, darker ones, about which we know little. Anton Ottenwalt, Spaun's brother-in-law, greatly admired Schubert and was captivated by the composer's intellectual and musical genius when Schubert visited Linz in 1825. In a letter to Spaun that year, Ottenwalt remarks that in Schubert's works, if not necessarily in the man, "the genius of divine creation reveals itself irreducibly through the passions of an ardently avid sensuality."[2]

Elizabeth Norman McKay, one of Schubert's most recent and thorough biographers, has explored Kenner's phrase regarding Schubert's "two natures," and has suggested that the composer suffered from cyclothymia, a mild form of manic depression.[3] This condition, which she believes ran in Schubert's family, would account for his well-documented changes in mood, productivity, and behavior, and goes a long way toward explaining the dark side of his life. Other commentators have long recognized Schubert's melancholy, depression, and "tragic perspective," but none has explored the clinical implications in quite such detail. McKay's proposal addresses, if not completely answers, too many questions to be quickly dismissed. Schubert's excessive drinking, his often not showing up for scheduled gatherings (both formal and informal) or abruptly disappearing from them, his unkempt physical appearance, his waves of phenomenal productivity contrasting with periods of utter inactivity (or severely reduced activity) – all this might be explained by what would today be diagnosed as depression.

Kenner's view of Schubert, even its binary language, resonates with many other remarks. Bauernfeld, for example, made several pertinent observations over the years:

> [Schubert] was able to divide his life between congenial work and pleasure. (1829; SMF 32)

> Schubert had, so to speak, a double nature, the Viennese gaiety being interwoven and ennobled by a trait of deep melancholy. [Schubert was] inwardly a poet and outwardly a kind of hedonist. (1857; SMF 45)

There slumbered in Schubert a dual nature. The Austrian element, uncouth and sensual, revealed itself both in his life and in his art . . . [It] appeared all too violently in the vigorous and pleasure-loving Schubert; there were also times when a black-winged demon of sorrow and melancholy forced its way into his vicinity – not altogether an evil spirit, it is true, since, in the dark, consecrated hours, it often brought out songs of the most agonizing beauty. But the conflict between unrestrained enjoyment of living and the restless activity of spiritual creation is always exhausting if no balance exists in the soul. (1869; SMF 233)

Mayrhofer likewise noted that Schubert's "character was a mixture of tenderness and coarseness, sensuality and candor, sociability and melancholy" (1829; SMF 14). And even the protective Spaun remarked the disparities, although without the negative connotations:

[Schubert] was unusually frank, sincere, incapable of malice, friendly, grateful, modest and sociable; sharing his joy but keeping his sorrow to himself. (1829; SMF 25)

Altogether, the world's judgment may blame him in many ways that he was not to be constrained by the conventions of society, where there was no intimate relationship to appeal to him, and that he had an elastic conscience where such duties were concerned, just as he would frequently break his promise to appear at some function held by high-placed patrons if he saw a prospect of spending the same hours at a subsequently arranged gathering of his friends or, more particularly, a summer's evening in the open air. This doubtless gave him the reputation here and there of having lacked social graces and education, and indeed of having been, artistic genius excepted, a quite insignificant personality. (1829; SDB 877–78)

[In the morning Schubert was] occupied with composition, aglow, with his eyes shining and even his speech changed, like a somnambulist . . . In the afternoon he was admittedly another person. (1858; SMF 138)

One area about which friends made extremely frequent remarks was Schubert's drinking. If McKay is correct in emphasizing

Schubert's depression and arguing that it only worsened over time, then use of alcohol as a sort of self-medication might not be unexpected. References to Schubert's drinking come not only in later accounts, but also in documents dating from his lifetime. Spaun even felt compelled to state that Schubert never drank to excess, which may exactly indicate that he sometimes did. He argued that Schubert's industrious habit of composing from early morning until lunch proved his dedication and that after such intense effort, the desire for friendly nocturnal discussions is entirely understandable. In any case, productivity, especially artistic creation, is not necessarily incompatible with heavy drinking; indeed, they may complement each other as different kinds of escape.

The general pattern of Schubert's mature life consisted of composition in the morning (he often smoked while writing), rest or walks in the afternoon, and evenings spent at theaters, at Schubertiades, with the reading society or, most often, with friends socializing in pubs. Sonnleithner, not much of a party person himself, dourly noted that "on such occasions midnight often passed unnoticed and pleasure was indulged to excess" (SMF 109). The circle tended to frequent a particular establishment for some months and then move on to a new one – some of their favorite haunts still exist. For practical reasons, a great many social activities took place in inns and taverns, rather than in private lodgings. (The importance of the Viennese café tradition would of course continue well into the twentieth century.) We do not know how much Schubert drank each night, no doubt it varied, but there are indications that it could be excessive, especially when he was depressed or confronted by people and situations with which he was not completely comfortable. Bauernfeld, who also defended Schubert against rampant charges of being a "drunken savage," nonetheless admitted that his friend "sometimes drank himself into a state of thorough-going tipsiness." Gerhard von Breuning and Josef Hüttenbrenner mention occasions when Schubert was drunk amid higher society: "Yesterday we had to carry our Schubert into another room; he had had too much to drink" (SMF 260, 255; cf. 191). Wilhelm von Chézy remembered that "when the juice of the vine glowed within him, he did not bluster or anything like that but liked to withdraw into a corner and give himself contentedly to silent rage, . . . while doing this he used to grin and screw up his eyes quite small" (SMF 261). It must have pained Schubert's friends to record such things about him, but enough did so that a clear pattern emerges. Spaun, ever the faithful and protective friend, lodged his protest: "There are so many references in [Kreissle's] biography to Schubert's love of wine . . . such repeated insinuations can hardly help giving rise to the view that Schubert was intemperate and addicted to drink, and this was by no means the case" (SMF 360).

Schubert indulged in various stimulants as well: he smoked pipe tobacco regularly and drank strong coffee (his friends did as well). McKay suspects that he may even have occasionally smoked opium, although this speculation is based on slim evidence, principally a passing reference to smoking a long Turkish water pipe.[4] We must be careful in exploring this area because modern associations with labels such as "alcoholic" and "substance abuser" probably do not do justice to Schubert's situation. And yet his use and abuse of caffeine, tobacco, and alcohol; his hedonism and sensuality; the manner in which he sought sexual gratification and release – these issues can no longer be repressed as they have been in the past. For one thing, there were consequences of this behavior that go beyond the probable cause of his illness and the continued decline of his health.

Beginning in the early 1820s, and accelerating as he aged, we find intensifying indications of Schubert's dissipation, stubbornness, irresponsibility, and occasional arrogance. According to Anselm Hüttenbrenner, Schubert "neglected his appearance, especially his teeth, and smelt strongly of tobacco" (SMF 70). An exceedingly common complaint was his failure to appear when and where he was expected. This behavior ranged from disappointing friends waiting for him at a pub to causing considerable annoyance and consternation by his absence from more important social occasions. Not that these disappearances were limited to a particular period during his illness;

they occurred throughout the 1820s. Schubert must have had his reasons, yet while his friends were generally understanding (though Schwind was particularly upset at one point in 1825 [SDB 424]) and excused his artistic idiosyncrasies, various patrons were offended and opportunities for advancement were jeopardized.

Schubert's arrogance and volatility is sometimes mentioned in letters and in various anecdotes. His Seminary classmate Anton Holzapfel wrote to Albert Stadler in 1822 that he rarely saw Schubert, "nor do we get along very well . . . His somewhat gruff manner stands him in very good stead and will make a strong man and ripe artist of him" (SDB 211). The anecdotes, not all of which may be accurate, tell of Schubert's flying into rages, especially in situations where alcohol would likely have been present. Some friends worried that Schubert's irresponsible behavior was hurting his career, that he was on "the wrong road." Those who had helped him get his first songs published were justifiably angry when he sold the rights outright to Diabelli for a handsome price, but not nearly for their true value. As Sonnleithner recalled, "This really rather ungrateful behavior on Schubert's part did not estrange him from us in any way; we regretted his weakness but continued to promote the performance and furtherance of his works." Kathi Fröhlich recalled that she felt herself "duty bound to give him a severe lecture, pointing out that his behavior and mode of life were far from commendable" (SMF 109, 255).

Many people at the time, and later, blamed Schober as a malignant influence. Already during Schubert's teenage years, there were occasional disparaging references to Schober's dubious behavior and to his unfortunate effect on others. In 1816, Spaun received a letter from his future brother-in-law Anton Ottenwalt musing about Schober:

What will become of him? It hurts me the most that I see this richly gifted, beloved, and blooming young man attacked in the most noble parts of his reason, without self-confidence, without youthful vigor, without joy and hope, looking toward the future in those years where a man should create his life's happiness . . . The blossom has been affected: from where shall the fruit come? It is not the single unhappy

> passion that brings him to this state . . . The evil lies deeper: it is the
> softness, the yielding, the gushing, the acting according to whims
> which does not know of self-deprivation, of the overcoming of
> obstacles, or of obedience . . . He will never find peace, he will drift
> through life empty and dissatisfied, will feel deeply and with sorrow
> what could or should have become of him.[5]

This analysis proved uncannily prescient: Schober, the eternal dilet-
tante, lived a long life and never amounted to much of anything. Of
regrets, he had plenty.

While some earlier friends had tired of his company, Schubert
wrote in November 1823, "Only you, dear Schober, I shall never
forget, for what you have meant to me no one else can mean, alas!"
(SDB 301). Others feared Schober's hold over Schubert; Vogl, in particular, objected strongly to his growing authority. After the eminent
singer had done so much to help launch Schubert's stage career, he
took offense that his protégé would waste his time writing *Alfonso* with
Schober, a text Vogl rightly realized was ineffective. Anton von Spaun
discussed the situation in a letter to his wife from 1822,

> Vogl is very embittered against Schober, for whose sake Schubert
> behaved most ungratefully toward Vogl and who makes the fullest
> use of Schubert in order to extricate himself from financial
> embarrassments and to defray the expenditure which has already
> exhausted the greater part of his mother's fortunes . . . Vogl says that
> altogether Schubert is quite on the wrong road. (SDB 230)

Vogl was also understandably disturbed, after helping to support
Schubert financially for years, that Schober could wield such power
and take such advantages. (This is the first we hear that Schubert gave
Schober money – perhaps he began to pay rent at some point; at the
time of Schubert's death he owed Schober money.)

Later in the century some acquaintances issued quite harsh ver-
dicts on Schober's "equivocal moral behavior" (SMF 62); Kenner in
particular, went so far as to call Schober "Schubert's seducer" and

10 Franz von Schober, oil painting by Leopold Kupelwieser (1822).

accused him of hastening his death. Kenner's diatribe makes one wonder about its underlying motivation, especially given their one-time close friendship. Kenner calls Schober "seductively amiable and brilliant . . . endowed with the noblest talents, [he was] a false prophet, who embellished sensuality in such a flattering manner." Kenner believed that

11 Josef von Spaun, oil painting by Leopold Kupelwieser (1835).

there reigned in [Schober's] whole family a deep moral depravity, so
that it was not to be wondered at that Franz von Schober went the
same way. Only he devised a philosophical system for his own
reassurance and to justify himself in the eyes of the world as well as to
provide a basis for his aesthetic oracle, about which he was probably
as hazy as any of his disciples; nevertheless, he found the mysticism
of sensuality sufficiently elastic for his own freedom of movement;
and so did his pupils. The need for love and friendship emerged with

such egotism and jealousy that to his adherents he alone was all, not
only prophet, but god himself, and apart from his oracles he was
willing to tolerate no other religion, no morals, no restraint.
(SMF 87)

Such characterizations about Schubert's closest friend are hardly
reassuring, and all the derogatory comments have tended to obscure
Schober's salutary contributions. His generosity over the years, his
affection and his desire to help Schubert, often provided the circumstances that made composition possible. Writing in 1876 to a nephew
of Schubert's, Schober made a rare comment about his friend: "I shall
always retain the eternally uplifting feeling of having freed this
immortal master from the constraint of [teaching] school, and of
having led him on his predestined path of independent, spiritual creation, and of having united with him in true and most intimate
friendship right up till his last breath" (SMF 208; cf. 210–11). Most
biographers would deny Schober the accuracy of his final claim, and
they relate that fear of infection stopped him from visiting the dying
composer.

Only rarely, as with the brief break with Vogl over Schober, does
anyone complain of Schubert's being less than a devoted and faithful
friend. In the eyes of posterity, Spaun's heartfelt words from 1858
summed up the human being: "Schubert was an affectionate son and
brother, and a loyal friend. He was a kind, magnanimous, good man.
May he rest in peace and thanks be to him for having beautified the
lives of his friends with his creations!" (SMF 140). Everyone who knew
Schubert clearly valued his generosity, modesty, and simplicity, and
precisely these qualities are what have blinded posterity to less admirable behavior and to darker demons. That Schubert often drank
immoderately, could be irresponsible and arrogant, and was sensual
and hedonistic – the image may be unfamiliar, but it is one that must
be taken seriously.

The temptation is almost irresistible to relate Schubert's "dual
nature" to his social and professional relations, and ultimately to his
music. We have seen the dichotomy between the formal social

gatherings Spaun mentions and the endless nights drinking with friends, the "pub crawlers"; between the high-minded moralism and purpose of the Linz Bildung Circle and the silliness of Vienna's Unsinnsgesellschaft; between the mornings spent isolated in concentrated composition and the evenings given over to communal pleasure. All of this points to an individual who personally, artistically, and professionally alternated between and mixed apparent opposites, even if he did not always successfully reconcile them. In "Mein Traum," Schubert wrote, "Whenever I attempted to sing of love, it turned to pain. And again, when I tried to sing of sorrow, it turned to love." He mulled over such oppositions as well in some scattered diary entries from March 1824. (As the originals are now lost, and the passages survive only in Bauernfeld's diary, they may not preserve Schubert's exact wording):

> Pain sharpens the understanding and strengthens the mind; whereas joy seldom troubles itself about the former and softens the latter or makes it frivolous.

> There is no one who understands the pain or the joy of others! We always imagine we are coming together, and we always merely go side by side. Oh, what torture for those who recognize this!

> What I produce is due to my understanding of music and to my sorrows; that which sorrow alone has produced seems to give least pleasure to the world. (SDB 336–37)

In fact, a surprisingly large number of Schubert's letters and other writings mix joy and sorrow ("Wohl und Weh," a familiar Romantic literary trope), and even when they do not explicitly declare this theme, they often demonstrate it by turning from melancholy topics to more hopeful ones.

The dual aspects of Schubert's character seem to correspond, perhaps almost too neatly, to contrasts repeatedly found in his music. Throughout Schubert's works, joy and sorrow meet in extraordinary ways. Haunting tonal juxtapositions, the turn from the carefree to the tragic (or the reverse), are hallmarks of Schubert's style from the beginning, and only become more mysterious and unsettling toward the end of his life. Even a procedure as commonplace as modulations between major and minor modes is used so often and so magically as to become one of Schubert's distinctive compositional fingerprints. Sometimes, as in *Erlkönig*, where the terror-filled world of the father and son is depicted in minor keys and the fantasy realm of the Erlking in major ones, Schubert has a discernible literary purpose; more often, however, the effect serves subtler aims, especially in his uncanny ability to make the major mode sound despairing.

Some critics find it difficult to reconcile Schubert's juxtaposition of elevated and popular styles, what we might today call "high" and "low." The first movement of the incomparable C Major String Quintet (D956) epitomizes Schubert's late style. The leisurely unfolding of beautiful melodies, the graceful slide into the flat mediant key for the melting second theme, and, once again, the characteristic fluctuations between major and minor modes – all these features represent a refinement of traits long favored by Schubert. The last movement, however, projects a more social and carefree attitude that some commentators consider disappointingly trivial in comparison with the first three movements. This movement seems to glance obliquely to neighboring Hungary and to project a surprising dancing gaiety. But such mixtures of moods over the course of a work, even within movements of a single composition, are typically Schubertian; few composers encompass such a range of genres, styles, and feelings. And indeed, within the last movement of the quintet, darker forces continue to lurk: the piece ends with a manic coda building to a dissonant fortissimo chord with a D-flat trill in both cellos, and then a final tonic inflected by a D-flat appoggiatura (a Neapolitan relationship that has already played an important role in earlier movements). The effect is overwhelmingly powerful, hardly carefree or affirmative, and forces us to reassess some of the preceding lightness.

Another duality, increasingly found in his mature music, invites attempts to relate unusual musical features to Schubert's personal life. He will abruptly interrupt a slow movement to insert a section of disturbing agitation and violence. The String Quintet is once again exemplary: the meditative serenity of the second movement attains the lyrical sublimity of Schubert at the very height of his powers, but upon this beauty intrudes one of his most terrifying outbursts of pain, even brutality; this is a gesture also seen in the slow movements of the "Great" C Major Symphony, the A Minor and G Major String Quartets, the Octet, and the late piano sonatas.[6]

In addition to the dual natures evident in Schubert's personality and social life, and to the suggestive contrasts so often found in his writings and his music, his career also demonstrates striking polarities, specifically the split between the "popular" and the "great" Schubert. This is evident in the staggeringly large quantity of songs and dances that Viennese publishers enthusiastically issued, while during his lifetime there appeared only one string quartet, one Mass, three piano sonatas, and no symphonies or operas. Balancing these spheres was a crucial professional challenge of Schubert's maturity.

The initial two years of Schubert's illness – 1823 and 1824 – were by no means lost artistically. Despite certain periods when he was simply not well enough to write, compositions poured forth. Schwind commented more than once that Schubert was being "superhumanly industrious." The traumatic experience of severe illness and the disturbing implications for his future inevitably changed him. Schubert movingly conveyed his intimations of mortality in some of his compositions from this troubled and troubling period, such as the darkly cast Piano Sonata in A Minor (D784), which was the first multi-movement secular work he had completed in years. *Die schöne Müllerin* and the D Minor String Quartet (D810) in some ways symbolically mark the beginning of Schubert's end, both compositionally – confirming that his years of apprenticeship were past – and biographically – showing a new maturity, seriousness, and artistic responsibility in the face of a possibly shortened life.

Die schöne Müllerin is the first of the two song cycles that set poems by Wilhelm Müller, a young contemporary poet from central Germany.

(It is unlikely that the composer and poet met, even though Müller traveled to Vienna in 1817.) Schubert composed other songs that he may have intended as a group and that possess some loose narrative or thematic thread, but this cycle and the later *Winterreise* present unified stories over the space of twenty and twenty-four songs respectively. Even if he largely failed in opera and oratorio, in the Müller cycles Schubert brilliantly achieved a large-scale narrative that established a lasting standard for the song cycle and that deeply influenced Schumann, Brahms, Mahler, and others.

According to Spaun and Schober, Schubert composed some of the *Müllerin* songs while in the hospital in 1823. He wrote the D Minor Quartet, known as "Death and the Maiden," the following year. Musicologist Susan Youens has explored the connection between sexuality and death in *Die schöne Müllerin* – how the sexual passion of the protagonist leads to his premature death by suicide – and has extended this connection to Schubert's own life when a sexually transmitted disease threatened his future.[7] The quartet has even more obvious mortal associations. While Schubert had previously written instrumental works based on earlier songs – such as the "Trout" Quintet and "Wanderer" Fantasy – one cannot help being struck by the significance of his return in March 1824 to his song *Death and the Maiden* of 1817, in which the solemn figure of death confronts an innocent youth with an offer impossible to refuse: "Give me your hand, you lovely, tender creature. I am a friend and come not to punish. Be of good courage. I am not cruel; you shall sleep softly in my arms."

Many other songs from this time also look toward death, but perhaps one should not read too much into the emotional or programmatic nature of these pieces. For one thing, Schubert could produce some of his sunniest creations during miserable times, such as dances (e.g. D783 and D790), partsongs, four-hand compositions, and the delightful one-act Singspiel *Die Verschworenen*, completed in April 1823. Moreover, we have just noted that Schubert continuously explored dualities in his music, contrasts between joy and sorrow, happiness and pain. Finally, his obsession with death can be found even in his earliest compositions. Songs such as *Der Vatermörder, Der Geistertanz*, and *Leichenfantasie*, all exhibit something other than a puerile fascination with the macabre; they reflect a pervasive Viennese cultural sensibility.

Schubert expressed his anguished state of mind not only in music but also through an unusually large number of philosophical ruminations in letters, diary entries, and even in one of his own rare poems, which he entitled "Mein Gebet" (My Prayer):

> Deeper longing's holy fears
> Want to live in fairer worlds,
> Wished to fill the darkened space
> With all-powerful dreams of love.
>
> Thou, great Father! Lend thy son
> To reward his deep despair,
> Finally as redemption's meal,
> Of thine love's eternal rays.
>
> See, undone in dust now lying,
> Victim to unheard-of grief,
> All my lifelong agony,
> Nearing final downfall.
>
> Kill it and myself do kill,
> Cast it all now in oblivion,
> And pure and potent life
> Let, O Lord, prosper then. (SDB 279)
>
> Tiefer Sehnsucht heil'ges Bangen
> Will in schön're Welten langen;
> Möchte füllen dunklen Raum
> Mit allmächt'gem Liebestraum.
>
> Großer Vater! reich'dem Sohne,
> Tiefer Schmerzen nun zum Lohne,
> Endlich als Erlösungsmahl
> Deiner Liebe ew'gen Strahl.

Sieh, vernichtet liegt im Staube,
Unerhörtem Gram zum Raube,
Meines Lebens Martergang
Nahend ew'gem Untergang.

Tödt' es und mich selber tödte,
Stürz' nun Alles in die Lethe,
Und ein reines kräft'ges Sein
Lass', o Großer, dann gedeih'n.

Schubert wrote this just a few months after the probable time of his
infection; it communicates his complete defeat while entreating a
greater power for redemption in a "pure and potent" state. This self-
examination and increasing resignation to a grim future were also
revealed in the March 1824 diary entries quoted earlier. The joy and
sorrow, pleasure and suffering, which Schubert had long explored in
his music, can increasingly be related to complex states of personal
experience. Schubert's prose registers despair and melancholy, as
well as a new maturity and acceptance of "the storms of life" (to use
the title a publisher would give some two decades later to his late
piano duo, the Allegro in A Minor, "Lebensstürme" [D947]). Even if
the medical treatments Schubert received, probably including applications of a highly poisonous mercury salve, were helpful, his view of
the world was nevertheless altered, and he apparently believed that his
time was limited. As tests to verify the healing of venereal diseases
were not yet available, one can reasonably speculate that Schubert
consciously embarked on his final creative stage, a period customarily
associated with the autumnal glow of later years, when he was only in
his mid-twenties.

As we have seen, during the early 1820s Schubert hoped that opera
would bring him fame and financial rewards. Even after the triumph
of Italian opera in Vienna, according to Bauernfeld, he continued to
write them despite the slim prospects of arranging performances.
One can only sympathize with the frustrations Schubert endured,
especially as after each disappointment would arise new glimmers of

hope. The great dramatic soprano Anna Milder, for example, wrote Schubert what amounted to a fan letter in December 1824, praising his songs, requesting more of them, and also expressing keen interest in his operas. One of the outstanding singers of her day, Milder had sung Leonore in all three versions of *Fidelio*. Haydn, Beethoven, and Schubert all greatly prized her art. Thus, her offer to help produce *Alfonso* in Berlin, where she now lived, must have heartened Schubert considerably, and he dispatched the score, together with the glorious song *Suleika II*, dedicated to her. Another disappointment: Milder replied that the libretto did not suit Berlin tastes, which inclined toward "grand tragic opera or French comic opera." Another glimmer of hope: wouldn't Schubert write a new opera for her, preferably in one act, on an oriental theme: "I should then do everything in my power to get the work staged" (SDB 409).

Before the unsuccessful intervention by Milder abroad, a series of mounting expectations and frustrating rejections had occurred at home. Despite Barbaja's concentration on Italian operas, he produced a few German works, which presented Schubert with some opportunities. Vienna's *Theaterzeitung* kept the public informed about the prospects of an opera apparently commissioned from Schubert. In October 1823 it reported, "The Kärntnertor-Theater is shortly to present the first grand opera by the highly-promising Schubert, the ingenious composer of *Erlkönig*: *Fierobras* [sic], after Calderón, by the Court Theater Secretary, Herr Kupelwieser. It is also said that Herr Schubert is composing a short opera." The paper soon elaborated: "The short Schubert opera is Castelli's *Die Verschworenen*. *Fierabras* will not be performed for the present." This information was retracted the following month: "*Fierabras*, which has been erroneously announced in these pages as having been withdrawn, is to appear as early as the end of January" (SDB 291, 300, 313).

Unfortunately, the retraction of this erroneous information itself proved erroneous; the first performance of *Fierabras* occurred only some eight decades later, as part of the Schubert centennial celebration of 1897. The three-act opera is set to a libretto by Josef Kupelwieser, Leopold's older brother and at the time secretary to the

Director of the Kärntnertor-Theater. A garbled affair once again, perhaps even less coherent than *Alfonso*, the plot concerns disputes, bat-
tles, intrigues, and love affairs between warring Franks and Moors.
Much of the music is remarkable – a compelling overture, delightful
choruses, and a haunting duet; and although dialogue is interspersed
between numbers (unlike *Alfonso*), there are long through-composed
sections as well.

Die Verschworenen (The Conspirators) is more modest. Ignaz Franz
Castelli, a civil servant, editor of a local periodical, and playwright,
based the one-act libretto on Aristophanes's *Lysistrata*. While *Fierabras*
passed the censorship office without problems, *Die Verschworenen* had
to be renamed *Der häusliche Krieg* (The Domestic War). Although
Schubert attributed the initial rejection of this charming concoction –
the only stage work of his to achieve any degree of posthumous popularity – to the fact that another composer had successfully set the same
libretto shortly before him, the reason was likely political. Once
again, Schubert's timing was off.

The far more disappointing failure of *Fierabras*, Schubert explained
to Schober, had to do with influence, connections, and Vienna's theatrical climate:

> With my two operas, things go very badly. [Josef] Kupelwieser has
> suddenly left the theater. Weber's *Euryanthe* turned out wretchedly
> and its bad reception was quite justified, in my opinion. These
> circumstances, and a new split between [Count] Pálffy [the owner of
> the Theater an der Wien] and Barbaja, leave me scarcely any hope for
> my opera. Besides, it would really not be a great stroke of fortune, as
> everything is done indescribably badly now. (SDB 301)

Weber had returned to Vienna in 1823, but *Euryanthe* did not enjoy
the success *Freischütz* had had just eighteen months earlier. Schubert
thought little of the opera, a view he expressed to Schober privately
and perhaps shared with Weber personally. Spaun recalled that Weber
had "shown the deepest respect and appreciation of Schubert's compositions" and tried to arrange for a production of *Alfonso* in Dresden.
Schubert's "frankness," however, caused problems when Weber

asked Schubert's opinion of Euryanthe and was told that while he admired the compositional skill, there was a "conspicuous lack of melody" and that he did not like it nearly as much as Freischütz (SMF 27; cf. 137, 366). Helmina von Chézy, who had written the libretto and for whom Schubert would soon compose incidental music to accompany her play Rosamunde, also referred to this falling out. Weber's faction was "indignant with the young composer, who had done nothing worse than express his opinion of Euryanthe in his frank Viennese way" (SMF 259). According to Chézy, Schubert alienated some of his supporters in this incident.

Near the end of 1823, one of Schubert's works did make it to the stage, although it was not a full-fledged opera. He had quickly composed the music for Rosamunde, a "Grand Romantic Drama in Four Acts with Choruses, Musical Accompaniment and Dances" in the fall of 1823. The work survived only two performances at the Theater an der Wien. But while Chézy's words were roundly panned, Schubert's music, the critics said, was "unanimously praised," and "left no doubt as to this popular master's genius" (SDB 313). Many commended the overture in particular, which had to be repeated. In fact, Schubert had not written a new overture, but rather had used the one for Alfonso; to confuse matters further, the overture to Die Zauberharfe was later published as Rosamunde, and it remains one of Schubert's most beloved works.

"German opera is finished altogether," a friend informed Schubert when Barbaja became the sole director of the opera. Schubert had arrived at the point at which, as Schwind assessed the situation in a letter, "the stage now seems altogether out of the question, at least as regards opera," and where endless vague hopes for productions abroad never materialized (SDB 440, 451). As well as responding to encouragement from Milder and perhaps also Weber, he pursued other leads for productions in Austria and northern Germany. After being urged, because of an amorous scandal, to leave the Kärntnertor-Theater at such an inopportune time, Josef Kupelwieser went to Graz where he was to become secretary to the theater and where he tried to get Fierabras staged. Schober wrote from Breslau that he might enlist

Gaspare Spontini, to whom he had access, for advice about *Alfonso* and also that he had contacted the prominent writer Ludwig Tieck, who was employed at the Dresden Court Theater. All Schubert could exclaim was, "What is to happen to my operas, Heaven knows!" (SDB 375).

Despite these frustrating disappointments, Schubert was still on the lookout for good librettos and continued to pursue opera projects to the end. In the summer of 1825, Schwind informed him that the poet Franz Grillparzer was interested in working on an opera for the Königsstadter Theater in Berlin, whose manager Grillparzer knew: "He repeated several times that he was really anxious about it" (SDB 426). Nothing came of this scheme either – a project Grillparzer had originally intended for Beethoven. Shortly after meeting Bauernfeld in 1825, Schubert and his new friend began to plan a collaboration. Schubert wanted to do *Die bezauberte Rose* (The Enchanted Rose), but Bauernfeld suggested *Der Graf von Gleichen*. Throughout his last years Schubert worked seriously on this opera, continuing to do so even after the censors rejected the libretto, on a medieval story involving bigamy. Dismal prospects still did not defeat Schubert. Moreover, despite the absence of any professional benefit, Schubert's opera projects, as McKay has observed, helped him "to bridge the gap between his more formal, classical compositions of the early years and the robust Romanticism he introduced into classical structures in his later years."[8]

Nevertheless by 1825 Schubert must have decided that it was time to get off this roller-coaster ride of soaring expectations and crushing let-downs. Opera was clearly not a feasible career path given the current management of Vienna's theaters; for the time being there was simply no stopping the Rossini craze. Schubert reformulated his hopes for subsistence and success by moving toward instrumental genres, and he realized that his efforts were best devoted to venues that offered greater possibilities for performance and publication than did the theater. In light of practical demands alone, debts must have mounted during his illness; Schubert needed to find new sources of income. The tangible successes, strong encouragements, and brilliant hopes of the early 1820s were now being frustrated by an oppressive combination of compositional crisis, professional obstacles, physical collapse, and psychic depression. Schubert was to experience a miserable period.

6 Poor Schubert: "Miserable reality"

Do not think that I am not well or cheerful, just the contrary. True, it is no longer that happy time when every object seems to us to be surrounded by a youthful glory, but a period of fateful recognition of a miserable reality, which I endeavor to beautify as far as possible by my imagination, thank God.

Schubert, letter to Ferdinand, 1824 (SDB 363)

After 1822, a surprising, yet revealing word crops up repeatedly in Schubert's letters: "miserable" (the word is almost the same in German). In addition to this letter to Ferdinand from the summer of 1824, Schubert elsewhere complains that "everything goes miserably," that such is "the lot of almost every sensible person in this miserable world. And whatever should we do with happiness, misery being the only stimulant left to us?" (SDB 300, 374). He confesses to often living "through days of great misery" (*sehr elende Tage*), complains that "it is very sad and miserable here," and so forth (SDB 375, 528). Whatever label psychiatrists today might apply, the "melancholic" side of Schubert's often "miserable" existence was a deeply felt reality.

In the aftermath of his illness many letters are quite bleak, and none more so than the famous one to Kupelwieser that opened the previous chapter. I consider this the key verbal document of Schubert's life, more important than any other surviving letter, "Mein

Traum," or his other scattered writings, because he not only offers a candid appraisal of his personal condition after enduring the worst of his health crisis, but also provides a declaration of the professional path he had planned for the future. (That Schubert sent the letter through a friend, and therefore had less need to worry about the authorities' reading it, may explain some of his frankness.) The complete letter reads:

31 March 1824

Dear Kupelwieser!

For a long time I have felt the urge to write to you, but I never knew where to turn. Now, however, [Johann Carl] Smirsch offers me an opportunity, and finally I can once again fully pour out my soul to someone. For you are so good and honest, you will be sure to forgive many things which others might take in very bad part from me.

In a word, I feel myself the most unhappy and wretched creature in the world. Imagine a man whose health will never be right again, and who in sheer despair over this ever makes things worse and worse, instead of better; imagine a man, I say, whose most brilliant hopes have perished, to whom the happiness of love and friendship have nothing to offer but pain, at best, whose enthusiasm (at least of the stimulating kind) for all things beautiful threatens to disappear, and I ask you, is he not a miserable, unhappy being?

"My peace is gone, my heart is sore, I shall find it never and nevermore," I may well sing again every day, and each morning but recalls yesterday's grief. Thus, joyless and friendless, I should pass my days, were it not that Schwind visits me now and again and shines on me a ray of those sweet days of the past.

Our society (reading society), as you probably know already, has done itself to death owing to a reinforcement of that rough chorus of beer-drinkers and sausage eaters, for its dissolution is due in a couple of days, though I have hardly visited it myself since your departure. [The pianist and music publisher Maximilian] Leidesdorf, with whom I have become quite well acquainted, is in fact a truly thoughtful and good fellow, but so hugely melancholic that I am almost afraid I owe him more than enough in that respect; besides, my affairs and his go badly, so that we never have any money. The opera [Fierabras] by your brother (who did not do any too well by leaving the theater) has been declared unusable, and thus no use has been made of my music. Castelli's opera, Die Verschworenen, has been set in Berlin by a local composer and received with acclamation. In this way I seem once again to have composed two operas for nothing. Of songs I have not written many new ones, but I have tried my hand at several instrumental works, for I wrote two string quartets and an octet, and I want to write another quartet; in fact, I intend to pave the way towards a grand symphony in that manner.

The latest in Vienna is that Beethoven is to give a concert at which he is to produce his new symphony, three movements from the new Mass, and a new Overture.

God willing, I too am thinking of giving a similar concert next year. I will close now, so as not to use too much paper, and kiss you 1,000 times. If you were to write to me about your present enthusiastic mood and about your life in general, nothing could more please,

Your faithful friend,

Frz. Schubert.

In this revealing letter, Schubert touches on every biographical theme of major significance for his maturity: health and future prospects, love and friendship, the decline of his social circle, nostalgia for a not-so-distant past, financial pressures, frustrations in seeking an opera career, the instrumental and performance path he wished to pursue, and a closing allusion to Beethoven, the composer who ultimately mattered most to him. Let us consider each of these areas so as to assess Schubert's position at this crucial juncture in his life and to prepare for our discussion of his phenomenal final years.

Writing to Schober the previous summer, Schubert had already expressed the fear that he would never fully recover. With Kupelwieser, he is more specific: not only will his health "never be

right again," but his actions are only making matters worse. Perhaps
this indicates some awareness of self-destructive tendencies, especially if continued drinking or other activities were threatening his
health. We cannot be sure to what behavior he alludes, and one wonders why he feels that while some might censure him, Kupelwieser
will surely "forgive many things." This is as direct a reference to dissipated living or to sexual illness as we get from Schubert himself.

In describing himself as the most "miserable, unhappy being,"
Schubert quotes Goethe's anxious lines from *Gretchen am Spinnrade*:
"My peace is gone, my heart is sore, I shall find it never and nevermore." The famous refrain of Schubert's first masterpiece now best
describes his own life: joyless, loveless, friendless. That he is deprived
of the "happiness of love" could refer to the hopelessness of serious
love affairs and the impossibility of marriage, given the nature of his
disease. "Friendless" seems antithetical to the apparent basis of
Schubert's friend-dominated existence, as well as to the core of his
posthumous image. Yet if we take him at his word and do not dismiss
the remark as self-pity, Schubert reveals something important about
the nature of his treasured relationships. Apparently only one person,
Schwind, provided friendship and visited him during his illness –
quite frequently, we may gather from the dispatches Schwind wrote
about his friend's condition.

The "poetic-musical-painting triumvirate" of Schober, Schubert,
and Kupelwieser that Spaun had inquired about in 1822 was now
made a quadrumvirate with Schwind. Seven or eight years younger
than the other three, Schwind was thrilled to join their company and
told Schober, "You have yourself ranked me with you and Schubert,
and I could not bear the delight of it . . . [this] means everything to me"
(SDB 324). Bauernfeld later recalled that "Schubert, who jokingly
called [Schwind] his beloved, took him completely to his heart" (SMF
239). Schwind was therefore Schubert's only close friend in Vienna
from the latter part of 1823 through the summer of 1825. Kupelwieser,
Schober, and Spaun were away, Senn had long since been exiled, the
friendship with Mayrhofer had cooled, and Bauernfeld only entered

the scene in 1825. Of all the many personalities who are mentioned in the correspondence and memoirs and whose faces appear in Schubertiade illustrations, those who mattered most were absent when Schubert wrote his letter. Apparently others could not fill their place; they did not share the same essential artistic and personal values.

Schubert found separation from his closest friends extremely distressing. In Zseliz once again some two months after writing to Kupelwieser, he informed Schober, "If only we were together – you, Schwind, Kupelwieser, and I – any misfortune would seem to be but a light matter; but here we are, separated, each in a different corner, and this is what causes my wretchedness" (SDB 374; cf. 370). When Schubert returned in mid October 1824, he lived at home for the last time, and then, in February, moved next door to Schwind into the so-called Fruhwirt-Haus near the Karlskirche. Schwind wrote Schober, "We meet daily, and as far as I can I share his whole life with him" (SDB 401).

Schubert recapitulates a theme to Kupelwieser that would only intensify in the coming years and that was appropriated in his posthumous reception: he grows nostalgic for their shared youth and for happy times of years not so long past. As he wrote to Schober on 21 September 1824 from Zseliz,

> I want to exclaim with Goethe: "who will bring back but an hour of that sweet time!" That time when we sat so snugly together and each, with motherly shyness, showed the others the children of his art, and awaited, not without worries, the judgment to be pronounced by affection and truth; that time when one inspired the other and thus united striving after the highest beauty enlivened us all. Now I sit here alone, deep in Hungary, where I unfortunately let myself be enticed a second time, without a single person with whom I can speak a sensible word.

We encounter a similar nostalgia time and again in Schubert's letters, as well as in the writings and illustrations of his friends. Spaun, away in Linz, informed Schober, "On the whole I am well content, only nothing can make me forget the happy, sociable hours I spent with you all, and which Schubert so often beautified; I fear they will never return so happily to me" (SDB 213). Thus we already find members of the Schubert circle, still in their twenties, looking back on their own youth. As we saw in the illustrations from chapter one, this gaze would grow more nostalgic after Schubert's death and would eventually help to characterize – and distort – an entire period of Viennese cultural life.

A specific consideration that Schubert communicates to Kupelwieser concerns the decline of the reading society (*Lesegesellschaft*). In December 1822, Schubert had informed Spaun that "our life together in Vienna is quite agreeable now. We hold readings at Schober's three times a week, as well as a Schubertiade" (SDB 248). The following season, after Schober's departure, meetings were held twice weekly at Ludwig Mohn's, beginning at seven o'clock in the evening and lasting some three or four hours. But Schubert complained to Schober that "our society, as indeed I had expected, has lost its central focus without you." Some new members joined and were given code names that indicate an affinity between private reading societies and the closed male clubs like the Unsinnsgesellschaft and the Ludlamshöhle (another group Schubert was on the verge of joining when it was disbanded in April 1826). According to Schubert, these initiates – "that rough chorus of beer-drinkers and sausage eaters" mentioned to Kupelwieser – made "the society only more insignificant instead of better. What is the good of a lot of quite ordinary students and officials to us?" (SDB 300). As Schubert predicted, meetings were soon suspended because they were too frequent, provoked too many disputes and, in the absence of Schober and Franz von Bruchmann, suffered from too little leadership. They would resume in 1828.

Personal rifts between friends around the same time raised tensions. When Schober left Vienna in August 1823 to pursue an acting career in Breslau, he was secretly engaged to Bruchmann's sister

Justina; Schwind acted as go-between, updating one about the other. Bruchmann disapproved of the relationship and finally exposed it, causing a lasting break. As Bruchmann wrote in his autobiography decades later, Schober "had the outrageous temerity to seek to sully one of the most precious jewels of my family."[1] Schubert, Schwind, and Schober found themselves at odds with former friends. Johanna Lutz, Kupelwieser's fiancée, wrote to him that Schubert and Schwind were in an "open feud" with Bruchmann and that he would probably be asked to choose for himself whom to support when he returned from Rome (SDB 406).

For his part, Schubert hoped that Schober's impending arrival would "bring a more lively and intelligent spirit into our circle again, much as it has shrunk" (SDB 432). And indeed, things did improve in late 1825 and 1826 with the reemergence of Schober, Kupelwieser, and Spaun, and the entrance of Bauernfeld as a new intimate. Spaun, who we must remember was nine years older than Schubert, ushered in a new era of socializing. Employed as a petty official at the state lottery and engaged to be married in April 1828, he hosted some of the most famous Schubertiades. In his diary, Franz von Hartmann described one such event from late 1826:

> I went to Spaun's, where there was a big, big Schubertiade . . . There was a huge gathering: the Arneth, Witteczek, Kurzrock and Pompe couples; Witteczek's mother-in-law; Dr. Watteroth's widow, Betty Wanderer, and the painter Kupelwieser with his wife; Grillparzer, Schober, Schwind, Mayrhofer and his landlord Huber, the tall Huber; Derffel, Bauernfeld, Gahy (who played gloriously à 4 mains with Schubert) and Vogl, who sang almost 30 splendid songs. Baron Schlechta and other court probationers and secretaries were also there. I was moved almost to tears . . . When the music was done there was grand eating and then dancing. (SDB 571–72)

In short, during the 1820s, Schubert's social life underwent a transition from fondly remembered student years, through a period of relative isolation brought on by illness and friends' absences, to a late time of mature union or reunion with friends old and new. Yet near the end, perhaps Schubert felt a fundamental aloneness even among his closest companions. Poor health had separated him from their idealized past, as well as from hopeful personal and professional futures. Even changes in Schubert's artistic preoccupations – his move away from Lieder and opera toward increasingly subtle kinds of instrumental and keyboard music – may have distanced him from those for whom literature was primary. Moreover, Schubert began to plumb darker realms in his music. *Winterreise* and the Heine songs display an alienation from all of life and the living. These were not pieces many Schubertiade participants could relate to as immediately as they had to much of Schubert's earlier music.

In his letter to Kupelwieser, Schubert alludes to financial difficulties. The issue of Schubert's material circumstances during his maturity will never be entirely sorted out. We are uncertain of all the income he received and of many of the expenses he incurred. In any case, within the context of a system of exchange and of communitarian sharing, and during a time of rife inflation, even accurate income figures would be misleading. I find the frequent attempts to give modern monetary equivalents virtually meaningless and in fact quite suspect – the agenda is usually to make Schubert seem destitute; only comparative figures are of some help. There was no doubt a certain amount of Bohemian exaggeration to the cries of pennilessness among members of the circle as they struggled to produce art while former classmates went off to comfortable (and rather undemanding) positions in the civil service. We must also remember that Schubert typically associated with persons from more prosperous backgrounds. Although he was much better off than the vast majority of Viennese, Schubert enjoyed neither the financial security nor the material amenities of his affluent friends, acquaintances, and patrons.

One reason that Schubert sought a theatrical alliance was to win its potentially handsome financial rewards. That he never had any money, as he tells Kupelwieser, was only true during certain periods. Debts must have mounted during his illness, because of doctors' fees and medications, but when compositions sold, Schubert would suddenly find himself with much more money than he had earned during an entire year as a school assistant. If Schubert was particularly hard pressed in March 1824, the situation changed some months later when he returned to Zseliz and could once again save his respectable salary. The following summer he made an extended, and no doubt costly, four-month journey with Vogl, and we may assume that the older singer again took care of many of the costs. (Vogl married, at an advanced age and much to everyone's surprise, in April 1826; this precluded further summer excursions.) Schubert hoped to meet Bauernfeld during the summer of 1826, but in the end explained, "I have no money at all, and altogether things go very badly with me. I do not trouble myself about it and am cheerful" (SDB 538).

We should make a clear distinction, therefore, between Schubert's ongoing financial insecurity and any state approaching true poverty. Schubert could not make money as a virtuoso performer, and he disliked teaching, especially in the morning when it would compete with his composing (SMF 109, 133). Yet he was generally well paid by publishers, particularly for his songs, he received money from commissions and dedications (such as a handsome amount from Count Moritz Fries, Beethoven's patron, for Gretchen am Spinnrade), and his public concert in 1828 brought in a large sum. All of this, however, was sporadic.

At various times Schubert explored the conventional road to financial stability: he applied for permanent jobs. We do not know for certain whether he sought or was offered a position as Deputy Court Organist, for which Schwind urged him to apply in 1825, and he may have tried for a job as a conductor or coach at the Kärntnertor-Theater the following year (Schindler provides a detailed account of Schubert's alleged audition [SMF 309–12]). In April 1826, Schubert wrote to the Emperor asking to be considered for the post of Vice Kapellmeister of the Court Chapel. Salieri had been Kapellmeister until his retirement in 1824, when his assistant Josef Eybler took over. Schubert enumerated his qualifications, including the fact that his

"name has become favorably known, not only in Vienna, but throughout Germany," and noted that he had "not the advantage of employment and hopes by means of an assured career to attain fully his
intended artistic goal" (SDB 520–21). After consideration of eight candidates, including Ignaz von Seyfried, Konradin Kreutzer, and
Anselm Hüttenbrenner, the position was given to Joseph Weigl, Chief
Conductor of the Court Theaters. Spaun later recalled that Schubert
wanted the job, but held no bitterness, for he considered Weigl worthy
(SMF 362). Taking any of these positions, of course, would have meant
drastic changes in Schubert's lifestyle, something he might not have
relished and for which there is good reason to believe he was tempera-
mentally ill-suited.

Finally, the vagaries of Schubert's financial situation must be
linked to his personal values and character. The general verdict as to
the latter is that Schubert was "an absolute child in money matters"
(SMF 134; cf. 109, 360). Perhaps he did not worry about his income so
long as he could compose, eat, drink, live where he wanted, and occasionally travel. Bauernfeld goes into some detail about the "commu-
nistic viewpoint" that prevailed among the friends, an account borne
out by other evidence:

> Hats, boots, neckerchiefs, even coats and certain other articles of
> clothing too, if they but chanced to fit, were common property . . .
> Whoever was flush at the moment paid for the other, or for the others
> . . . Naturally, among the three of us [Schubert, Bauernfeld, and
> Schwind], it was Schubert who played the part of a Croesus and who,
> off and on, was swimming in money, if he happened to dispose of a
> few songs or even of a whole cycle . . . To begin with there would be
> high living and entertaining, with money being spent right and left –
> then we were broke again! In short, we alternated between want and
> plenty. (SMF 228)

As is typical throughout Schubert's writings and music, sorrow and
sadness eventually turn to joy and optimism. Even if the first part of
Schubert's letter to Kupelwieser is depressed and depressing, reflect-
ing a sense of personal hopelessness and resignation, it closes with a

more sanguine discussion of recent compositions and designs for his professional future. This may provide a crucial insight into Schubert's psychological make-up. In other writings as well, he remarks that everything is miserable, that only music makes matters better. If we can speculate about his use of alcohol as self-medication, there is even more reliable evidence that industriousness, creativity, and the arts offered relief from melancholy. Spaun assures us that music was Schubert's consolation at the Seminary, Mayrhofer relates how composing sustained him during his years as a school assistant, and Schubert's own letters repeatedly profess that music cures his misery. *An die Musik* became one of his most famous songs, and it apparently held special importance for the composer. Easy as it is to dismiss Schober's sentimental poem, its tribute to the ability of music to brighten "dark hours" and transport one "to a better world" should perhaps be taken seriously – and literally. This was a hymn of thanks with which Schubert strongly identified; he copied it out on several occasions.

Schubert's lament to Kupelwieser that his "most brilliant hopes have perished" is especially remarkable because this formulation eerily prefigures the epitaph that would adorn his grave just four years later – Grillparzer's famous words that praise the wonders Schubert had created while mourning the loss of the "more splendid hopes" that might have been. Illness had put Schubert out of public view for a while after considerable exposure during 1820 and 1821, yet his supreme creative accomplishments were, in fact, some years off. Even if Schubert was depressed about what he perceived to be the loss of these bright opportunities and was additionally frustrated by the failures of the theater projects, he nonetheless formulated new compositional and professional plans: chamber music would "pave the way towards a grand symphony," and a high-profile public concert would finally spotlight his works to a much wider audience.

Schubert also informs Kupelwieser about two string quartets he had just written. The A Minor Quartet (D804), whose second movement quotes the "Entr'acte" in B-flat from *Rosamunde*, had been finished at the beginning of the month and premiered at the Gesellschaft der Musikfreunde two weeks later, on 14 March 1824, in one of Ignaz Schuppanzigh's subscription concerts. (Beethoven's Septet, Op. 20, was the other work on the program.) This proved the only occasion when an entire quartet of Schubert's was performed in public during his lifetime. While the realities of the Viennese theater scene had thwarted certain plans, an important change in the the professional presentation of chamber music now worked to Schubert's benefit. Nearly two decades earlier, Beethoven's patron, Count Rasumovsky, had requested that Schuppanzigh assemble the finest string quartet in Europe.[2] Together with Louis Sina, Franz Weiss, and Josef Linke, he presented private as well as subscription concerts. In December 1814, however, Rasumovsky's palace burned to the ground, and Schuppanzigh left Vienna, eventually settling in Russia. His return in 1823, and the reconstitution of his quartet with Weiss, Linke, and Karl Holz, inaugurated a glorious new era of chamber music, whose significance for Schubert should not be underestimated.

Beyond Schuppanzigh's promotion of Schubert's music at prominent concerts, their personal association must have had momentous musical consequences about which we can only speculate. Schuppanzigh was the principal performer to whom Beethoven turned in his final years (the composer called him "Falstaff" because of his obesity), not only for the late quartets, but also for his last public academy – the première of the Ninth Symphony that Schubert so eagerly mentions to Kupelwieser. Schuppanzigh was therefore an important common friend of both composers during their final years and a resource from whom Schubert could get to know Beethoven's late music even before it was performed and published. In addition, Schuppanzigh's prestige and the opportunities he provided for Schubert's works to share the limelight with Beethoven's at prestigious concerts helped the young composer achieve a new level of recognition and stature.

Six months after Schuppanzigh presented the A Minor Quartet, Maximilian Josef Leidesdorf – the melancholy publisher in straightened financial circumstances whom Schubert mentions spending time with – released the work as the first of "Trois Quatuors" Op. 29, No. 1. As Schubert informed Kupelwieser, he intended to compose three quartets, which Leidesdorf must have agreed to issue as Op. 29, Nos. 1–3. The publication of such a formidable set would have been relatively unusual at the time and would inevitably have invited comparison with Beethoven's famous triad, Op. 59, the "Rasumovsky Quartets." The A Minor, however, remained the only quartet published during Schubert's lifetime.

Schubert also mentions the D Minor Quartet, "Death and the Maiden" (D810), written the same month as the Kupelwieser letter. Franz Lachner, perhaps not reliable in this instance, states that Schuppanzigh found the work too difficult (SMF 289; cf. 372). The Octet (D803), commissioned by Count Ferdinand Troyer, steward to Archduke Rudolph and a prominent clarinettist, also dates from Schubert's miraculously productive months at the beginning of 1824, and is clearly modelled on Beethoven's popular Septet, Op. 20. Schuppanzigh read through the Octet at Troyer's apartment in the Graben that spring and presented the public première in his last subscription concert of 1827. That concert, just a month after Beethoven's death, consisted of just two other works: Beethoven's song cycle *An die ferne Geliebte* and an arrangement of the "Emperor" Concerto for two pianos and string quartet. (Carl Czerny was one of the pianists.)

In the A Minor and D Minor Quartets, and in the Octet, as well as in the "Wanderer" Fantasy and some of the piano compositions, Schubert once again makes use of earlier songs, dances, and even parts of stage pieces. He "recycled" and reinterpreted his own music throughout his career, and the phenomenon, which occurs frequently in slow movements in pieces from the mid and late 1820s, and often in the form of variations, is of musical, professional, and biographical interest. Schubert's lyricism permeates all the genres in which he composed and is of course a distinguishing feature of his instrumental works. Whereas Beethoven tended to explore exhaustively the possibilities of small motives, Schubert usually preferred a more leisurely

Oſtermontag den 16. April 1827

wird

das letzte

Abonnement ⸗ Quartett

des

Ignaz Schuppanzigh,

unter den Tuchlauben, zum rothen Igel (im kleinen Ver⸗
ein⸗Saale) Nachmittags von halb 5 bis halb 7 Uhr,
Statt haben.

Vorkommende Stücke:

1. Neues großes Octett für 5 Saiten⸗ und 3 Blas⸗Inſtrumente,
   von Herrn Schubert.

2. An die ferne Geliebte. (Ein Liederkreis für eine Singſtimme
   und Clavier⸗Begleitung, von Beethoven.

3. Großes Clavier⸗Concert (aus Es dur), von Louis van
   Beethoven, arrangirt für zwey Pianoforte und Quartett⸗Beglei⸗
   tung, gefälligſt vorgetragen von Herrn Carl Czerni und Herrn
   von Pfaller.

Eintrittskarten ſind auf dem Graben, in der Kunſthandlung des Herrn
T. Haslinger (vormahls Steiner & Comp.) zu haben.

12 A program for the last of Ignaz Schuppanzigh's subscription concerts for
the 1827 season, which saw the première of Schubert's Octet (a work
directly modeled on Beethoven's Septet, Op. 20), Beethoven's song cycle An
die ferne Geliebte, and his "Emperor" Piano Concerto, arranged for two
pianos and string quartet.

and expansive approach. His infusion of actual songs into a wide
range of instrumental works testifies to a sovereign lyric sensibility. A
manifest musical link between his earlier career as the Liederfürst and
his mature ambitions in large-scale works is audible in the incorporation of the former into the latter. Not only did small pieces help
Schubert build large compositions, but his fame and popularity in the
"popular" genres also helped prepare the public for "great" instrumental works. At the very least, here was an effective promotional

device: take a well-known song and reuse it in an instrumental work. Even if Schubert was sometimes acting unconsciously, such transformations connected naturally with the culture of variations of beloved tunes and of arrangements that so dominated his era.

Because of the association with specific texts, Schubert's self-quotations raise aesthetic issues concerning expressive content. A listener who knows the words to Der Wanderer, Der Tod und das Mädchen, and Die Götter Griechenlands may find keys to the meanings of the instrumental compositions in which these songs appear. The possible autobiographical implications of the "Death and the Maiden" Quartet have already been mentioned. The quotations in the A Minor Quartet and the Octet from Die Götter Griechenlands, written in 1819, are equally suggestive. The melody to the words "Beautiful world, where are you?" appears in both works.[3]

Although no mention is made to Kupelwieser, Schubert was also re-engaged with writing and publishing large keyboard compositions. In the "Wanderer" Fantasy, written at the onset of his illness in late 1822 and published the next year, Schubert created one of his most innovative forms, as well as his most virtuosic display. (The attraction the piece held for Liszt, who orchestrated it and performed it frequently, is hardly surprising.) The title, first applied long after Schubert's death, derives from his well-known song Der Wanderer, a melody which appears in the slow movement and which provides the core for the subtle manipulations of a few melodic and rhythmic ideas. The ingenuity of its thematic transformations and of the formal architecture, which suggests four movements merged into one, strongly influenced later composers.

In the 1810s, Schubert had written some fifteen piano sonatas (not all completed); he did not return to the genre until 1823 with the somber A Minor Sonata (D784). The so-called Reliquie Sonata in C Major (D840), another of Schubert's superb unfinished works, dates from two years later, and was soon followed by three more (A Minor, D845; D Major, D850; G Major, D894). These mature sonatas (only the miraculous last three, composed shortly before his death, remained to be written) display a further side of Schubert's professional aspirations and creative mastery. They offered somewhat limited possibilites for exposure because the piano recital as we know it today did not yet exist, and sonatas were very rarely performed in public. They did turn up, however, in salon settings; Schubert mentioned the final three in a letter to the publisher Heinrich Albert Probst: "I have played the sonatas with much success in several places" (SDB 811). The three completed sonatas from the mid 1820s were published, by different firms, in the space of two years (1825–26), and they attracted a relatively large number of reviews. All told, only a dozen or so really substantive articles on Schubert's music appeared during his lifetime, and these piano sonatas received more attention than any of his other published work save the Lieder. Although the general verdict was extremely supportive, the tone, particularly from journals outside Vienna, could sometimes be a little patronizing. Schubert was gently chastised for excesses – as he often was for the piano accompaniments of the Lieder – and for his harmonic adventures. Yet Schubert, who surely read this criticism, must have been encouraged. Two words appear frequently: *original* and *Beethoven*; he was praised for the former and repeatedly compared to the latter.[4]

Another large keyboard work from mid decade shows even more ambition – the "Grand Duo" for piano four-hands. Indeed, Robert Schumann later commented in a famous review: "I regarded it as a symphony arranged for the piano until the original manuscript which by his own hand is entitled 'Sonata for Four Hands' taught me otherwise."[5] The four-movement work is one of the longest Schubert ever wrote; indeed, just as Schumann took it for a symphony in disguise, the piece was later orchestrated by others, most notably by Joseph Joachim. Yet for all the wonders contained in Schubert's sonatas and the "Grand Duo," and however useful the sonatas proved in broadening his reputation through publication and reviews, Schubert was more concerned with chamber music because of its public prominence and, more importantly, because it helped "pave the way towards a grand symphony."

The "Grand Duo" was Schubert's significant work from the summer of 1824, his second trip to Zseliz. The following summer he made the extended four-month tour with Vogl to Steyr, Linz, Gmunden, Salzburg, and Gastein. Schubert informed his friends that he was writing a symphony, apparently the grand project for which he had been preparing. A famous Schubert legend is that this symphony is lost. The details are too complicated to recount completely here, but suffice it to say that the so-called Gastein Symphony is none other than the "Great" C Major Symphony (D944), traditionally thought to date from 1828. Not only is there considerable stylistic and circumstantial confirmation to support this claim, but also scientific evidence of the handwriting and watermarks of the manuscript.[6] This new chronology is of considerable importance because it shows that the optimistic and extroverted "Great" Symphony came from one of the happiest and most productive times of Schubert's life and not from his darker and more introspective last year. At the same time, the violent interruption in the slow movement points to comparable moments encountered in many of the later works.

Spaun and Bauernfeld relate that Schubert had a "very special predilection" for his "Grand Symphony" written at Gastein (SMF 24, 31). Certainly the scene of its composition was ideal. In the longest letters he ever wrote, intended for his brother Ferdinand but never sent, Schubert described the inspiring beauty of his surroundings, particularly near the mountains and lakes of Gmunden. Die Allmacht, also written on the journey, captures his pantheistic belief in the awesome power of the Almighty as experienced in nature. This C major song may be considered a companion piece to the vast expanse and majesty of the orchestral work. Only Beethoven had written a longer and more ambitious symphony before this, the mighty Ninth, whose "Ode to Joy" theme Schubert briefly quotes in his own last movement (measures 386ff).

Prospects for imminent performance of the work seemed good. Even while Schubert was still traveling with Vogl, Schwind wrote from Vienna, "About your symphony we may be quite hopeful. Old Hönig is dean of the law faculty and as such is to give a concert. That will afford a better opportunity of having it performed; indeed we may count on it" (SDB 451). But the work was not played at this concert, given on 30 April 1826, nor at any other. In October, Schubert presented it to the Gesellschaft der Musikfreunde with this explanation: "Convinced of the Society's noble intention to support any artistic endeavor as far as possible, I venture, as a native artist, to dedicate to them this, my symphony, and to commend it most politely to their protection" (SDB 559). They voted to give him 100 florins, "not as a fee," secretary Raphael Georg Kiesewetter explained, "but as a token of the Society's sense of obligation towards you, and with the gratitude with which it acknowledges the interest you have shown it" (SDB 560). Soon afterward the Society paid two copyists to make orchestral parts so that the work could be played. Sonnleithner tells us that the conservatory orchestra read through the symphony at some point, but we do not know when (SMF 431).

Perhaps with thoughts of performance or publication in mind (he repeatedly mentioned the symphony to publishers), Schubert returned to the work in 1828 and redated it at that point. Indeed, the primary reason for the misunderstanding about the "Gastein"/C Major Symphony is the date – March 1828 – written in Schubert's hand. This is what confused Sir George Grove and so many others. Certainly the idea of a "lost" symphony is very attractive – it might be found some day – and seems especially appropriate in connection with Schubert because so much was "lost" in a figurative sense by his early death. One can understand why Grove, who unearthed Schubert compositions during visits to Vienna in the 1870s, could easily be seduced into searching for a lost symphony, even on rather flimsy grounds. And once the legend was born, it took on a life of its own; even the sober Otto Erich Deutsch ambivalently supported the idea and went so far as to assign the "Gastein" a number: D849.

After his return to Vienna in 1825, living again in the Fruhwirt-Haus, Schubert appears to have been less productive for some time, although it may just seem that way because we can not be sure how much work remained to be done on the symphony, or what the exact

13 Wilhelm August Rieder's famous watercolor of Schubert (1825).

chronology was of some other large projects, such as the Piano Trio in B-flat (D898). A welcome circumstance was Spaun's moving back to Vienna after nearly five years' absence. There, he recalled finding Schubert "in the full flowering of his talent. At last he was finding more recognition, and he was receiving payment for his works" (SMF 136). There are many signs of Schubert's rising stature. While still away with Vogl, he was elected one of twenty deputies to the representative committee of the Gesellschaft der Musikfreunde. (Honors had already come in 1823 from the Music Societies in Graz and Linz.) Artist Wilhelm August Rieder painted the well-known portrait of his friend in May 1825, and an engraving after it by Johann Nepomuk Passini was offered for sale later that year. The *Wiener Zeitung* announced, "The extremely good likeness of the composer FRANZ SCHUBERT ... the composer of genius, sufficiently well known to the musical world, who has so often enchanted listeners with vocal compositions in particular, appears here in a speaking likeness, and we therefore believe we have presented Schubert's numerous friends and admirers with a welcome gift" (SDB 478).

Schubert ends his letter to Kupelwieser with gossip about Beethoven's impending concert, which would see the première of the Ninth Symphony, three movements of the Missa solemnis, and the Overture to the Consecration of the House. Schubert expresses the hope that he too might be able to present a concert devoted entirely to his compositions. His active quest for performances and publications (Schober urged him to launch a publicity campaign) shows new energy with respect to his public career. While others had negotiated on his behalf in the past, Schubert now took matters into his own hands. Most importantly, he had reached the point where he could and would acknowledge his large-scale compositions rather than disparage or disavow them: "this, my symphony," he tells the Gesellschaft der Musikfreunde. A letter to a publisher contains a similar reference to "a symphony" he has written, as if all the earlier ones did not exist or matter. And in many ways, they did not.

To conclude our discussion of Schubert's letter to Kupelwieser, let us return to his passing mention of love. When Schubert links love and friendship in a single phrase, saying that their joy now causes him only pain, we cannot be sure whether he is alluding to physical or platonic love. Certainly his illness greatly diminished any chance of a conventional marriage. In an 1825 letter to his parents, Schubert inquired after his brother Karl's recent marriage and the prospects of children. Schubert, for his part, declared, "I renounce it myself" (SDB 436). Regardless of the exact nature of Schubert's libidinal desires, there is ample evidence in his letters, as well in writings of others in the circle, that the composer disdained many aspects of traditional bourgeois life, particularly regular employment, institutional religion, conformist thinking, and marriage. Freedom – political, personal, professional, and creative – was extremely important to the way Schubert sought to live his life.

Recent articles by musicologist Maynard Solomon argue that Schubert was probably not interested in marriage in any case because his primary erotic orientation was homosexual. Among the "separate strains of evidence" Solomon discusses are "widespread reports of his dissipation, the paucity of his reported female love-interests, his failure to marry, his renunciation of fatherhood, his passionate male friendships, his domestic arrangements, the rapturous relationships among the young men of the Schubert-Schober circle, and a series of oblique references in correspondence, memoirs, and diaries."[7] One such coded allusion Solomon finds in an August 1826 entry in Bauernfeld's diary: "Schubert ailing (he needs 'young peacocks,' like Benvenuto Cellini!)" (SDB 548). Solomon speculates that this may indicate that Schubert sought out young male prostitutes in Vienna's *Halbwelt*, although others contend that this passage refers to a treatment for his syphilitic condition.

So much evidence is lost – or remains to be unearthed. Although we have considerable information about much amorous activity of others in the circle, about Schubert's attentions throughout these troubled years there are only scattered hints. During his second stay in Zseliz, Schubert alludes in a letter to a terrible yearning for Vienna "in spite of the certain attractive *star*" (SDB 370). Perhaps he is referring to Pepi Pöckelhofer, the chambermaid he had mentioned in a letter six years earlier. The more likely candidate, many feel, is Caroline Esterházy, the younger of the two countesses he was charged with teaching; she was now about to turn nineteen (Schubert was twenty-seven). In any case, Schubert's letters show that he was most concerned about being separated from his male friends and that he deeply resented his absence from Vienna's cultural life.

Whatever the causes and aftermath of his illness, the decline of the circle, or the difficulties of his career, the emotional centers of Schubert's existence were his creative life and his closest friends. In the words of one of his first obituaries, Schubert "lived solely for art and for a small circle of friends" (SMF 10). As for matrimony, I find most suggestive a musical and figurative union growing ever stronger during the 1820s, one that posterity would perpetuate in fascinating ways – the eternal marriage with Schubert's Immortal Other: Beethoven.

7 Late Schubert: "Who shall stand beside Beethoven?"

He was an artist . . . Who shall stand beside him?

Franz Grillparzer, Funeral oration for Beethoven, 1827

During his final two years Schubert created his supreme music, enjoyed his broadest public recognition, and could realistically look toward growing professional success. That this period also spans Beethoven's last illness and the twenty months separating their deaths is, I think, more than just a coincidence. After the passing of his artistic father figure, Schubert produced a sustained series of masterpieces unprecedented in his career; at the same time, he sought public exposure with increasing urgency. Redoubling efforts begun some years earlier, Schubert contacted publishers himself, performed in public, and planned highly visible concerts. Beethoven's death left a gaping void in the musical world, and we patronize Schubert if we imagine he would not have considered himself worthy of assuming his great predecessor's mantle. He was now prepared.

When in March 1827 Schubert participated as a torchbearer in Beethoven's funeral, he heard a question – a challenge, in fact – posed in Franz Grillparzer's celebrated oration: "He was an artist . . . Who shall stand beside him?" What must Schubert, recently turned thirty and himself in precarious health, have thought hearing the words of his literary friend read in tribute to his musical hero? Grillparzer invoked the names in the pantheon of German musical genius as he welcomed Beethoven to their company. What did Schubert make of the question of who would be the next immortal composer? And yet, as the question was being posed, the answer incarnate stood there among the mourners and himself was soon to die.

Although it is almost inconceivable that Beethoven and Schubert did not meet on various occasions, the exact nature of their personal relations remains unclear. Geographical, social, and professional circumstances in Vienna provided ample opportunity for encounters, and yet the evidence is both sparse and contradictory. Two individuals best in a position to know gave flatly opposing accounts. Ferdinand Schubert stated that Schubert "met [Beethoven] frequently" (SMF 37) while Spaun recounted that "Schubert often lamented, especially at the time of Beethoven's death, how much he regretted that the latter had been so inaccessible and that he had never spoken to Beethoven" (SMF 366). Kreissle reported that "several of Schubert's most intimate friends, who are still living, cannot remember any more than a chance interview between the two composers."[1]

After moving to Vienna in 1792, Beethoven remained for the rest of his life. The two composers lived and worked in a tightly knit musical culture, sharing many of the same supporters, publishers, performers, and acquaintances. Although little connection existed between their intimate friends, and despite Beethoven's increasing withdrawal from the public eye after the time of the Congress of Vienna, their orbits nevertheless overlapped. When Schubert published his first substantial instrumental composition – the *Eight Variations on a French Song*, Op. 10, for piano duet – in 1822, the work carried an effusive dedication to Beethoven from "his Worshiper and Admirer Franz Schubert." Of the many stories describing personal encounters between them, two concern this piece. The none-too-reliable Anton Schindler, who knew both composers, reported in 1860 that Schubert and the publisher Diabelli personally delivered the variations to Beethoven, that Schubert's shyness incapacitated him from speaking to the master, and that Schubert "lost control of himself" when

VARIATIONEN

uber ein französisches Lied für das

Piano-Forte auf vier Hände

VERFASST UND DEM

Hr. Ludwig van Beethoven

Zugeeignet von seinem Verehrer und Bewunderer

Franz Schubert.

№ 996   10ᵗᵉˢ Werk   Pr. 1/ſt C.M
                                    2/ſoᵗ W.W.

Eigenthum der Verleger.

Wien bey Cappi und Diabelli, Graben № 1133.

14 Cover of Schubert's *Eight Variations on a French Song*, Op. 10, which he dedicated to Beethoven in 1822.

Beethoven gently pointed out a mistake in the harmony (SMF 325). Josef Hüttenbrenner, on the other hand, related in 1857 that Schubert tried to deliver the composition, but that Beethoven was not at home at the time. Nevertheless, Hüttenbrenner asserted that the variations "received Beethoven's full approval" and that "Beethoven played them almost everyday with his nephew for a period of months" (SMF 75).

Other accounts are less specific. For some years Beethoven had held court, so to speak, a few mornings each week at the publishing house of Steiner & Co. Schubert was frequently there, we are told, although probably a silent presence. The most tantalizing report of contact concerns Beethoven's final days. Their common friend, Anselm Hüttenbrenner, insisted, "I know for an absolute fact that Professor Schindler, Schubert and I visited Beethoven at his sickbed about a week before he died" (SMF 66). But Schindler recorded no such meeting, nor did anyone else (save Anselm's brother Josef), and in any event, the story only appeared decades after the alleged encounter occurred.

Beethoven died during a violent storm on the afternoon of 26 March. His funeral was held three days later. Among the many corroborating accounts of that event, an official description documents Schubert's participation in the ceremony, together with Vienna's artistic luminaries:

> The ends of the pall (not the points) were taken by the eight Kapellmeister – Eybler, Hummel, Kreutzer, Seyfried on the right; Gänsbacher, Gyrowetz, Weigl, Würfel on the left – the honor escort of the sleeping master. They carried candles wrapped in crepe. On both sides of the coffin came the torchbearers: Anschütz, Bernard, Blahetka, Joseph Böhm, Castelli, Karl Czerny, David, Grillparzer, Konrad Graf, Grünbaum, Haslinger, Hildebrandt, Holz, Kaller, Krall, Lannoy, Linke, Mayseder, Meric, Merk, Mechetti, Meier, Paccini, Piringer, Rodicchi, Raimund, Riotte, Schoberlechner, Schubert, Schickh, Schmiedl, Streicher, Schuppanzigh, Steiner, Weidmann, Wolfmayer, and others, with lily bouquets adorning their shoulders. The torches were decorated with flowers.[2]

Biedermeier Vienna loved a good funeral, and Beethoven's was one of its most imposing. Descriptions of the splendid occasion disagree as to how great a multitude of mourners joined the procession from the parish church in the Alsergrund to Währing Cemetery. *Der Sammler* reported 10,000, while Gerhard von Breuning doubled the number, and Schindler tripled it. In Franz Stöber's well-known watercolor, Beethoven's casket is overwhelmed by the throng – another indication of the magnitude of this day when theaters closed and the city lamented the loss of her premier artist.

As only priests were permitted to speak at the consecrated ground of the grave site, Vienna's foremost actor, Heinrich Anschütz (a friend of Schubert's), stood in front of the cemetery to deliver Grillparzer's oration. The eloquent address grieves over the passing of a great man, which concludes a magnificent epoch: "The last master of tuneful songs, the organ of soulful concord, the heir and amplifier of the

15 Franz Stöber's watercolor of Beethoven's funeral procession on 29 March 1827. Along with other prominent cultural figures, Schubert was a torchbearer at this occasion.

immortal fame of Handel and Bach, of Haydn and Mozart, is now no more, and we stand weeping over the riven strings of the harp that is hushed." Another passage alludes to a genius who "yet lives – and may his life be long!" This unnamed master – Goethe, of course – was later thought to be Schubert, but in 1827 no one would have considered pairing the relatively obscure composer with Beethoven as the exemplary artists of their age. Indeed, seven years later, when Schubert's supporter Raphael Georg Kiesewetter wrote an important general history of music, he justly characterized the time as the "Era of Beethoven and Rossini"; Schubert goes entirely unmentioned in Kiesewetter's book. It would take many years for this to be called the "Era of Beethoven and Schubert."[3] My point is that only one person attending Beethoven's funeral could have known who would follow him, who would share the crown of the epoch – and that was Schubert himself.

Kreissle's biography recounts the oft-told story of Schubert's activities later that day. He went with musician friends Franz Lachner and Benedikt Randhartinger to the Mehlgrube Inn, where he filled two wine glasses. With the first, he toasted the memory of Beethoven, and with the second, whoever among the three of them was destined next to die – which was, of course, Schubert the following year. Not surprisingly, this sentimental story is apocryphal. Only in the twentieth century did a diary entry by Fritz von Hartmann supply reliable information: "Went to the Castle of Eisenstadt [Tavern], where I remained with Schober, Schubert, and Schwind until almost 1 AM. Needless to say, we talked of nothing but Beethoven, his works and the well-merited honors paid to his memory today" (SDB 623). Even if the deathbed encounter between Beethoven and Schubert never occurred, Schubert's participation in the funeral must have had a profound impression on him, especially in view of his own debilitating illness. Spaun later recalled that Beethoven's "death shocked [Schubert] very deeply. Did he, perhaps, have a premonition of how soon he would follow him and rest at his side?" (SMF 137).

Schubert's fully mature and most ambitious compositional projects, as we have seen, had begun some years earlier. By the time Beethoven died, he had published the A Minor String Quartet and was hoping for the imminent release of those in D Minor and G Major; three piano sonatas had appeared, and the steady flow of smaller keyboard pieces for two and four hands advanced. In the realm of the Lied, Schubert's greater ambition is evident in his cultivation of the song cycle. After *Die schöne Müllerin*, published in 1824, Schubert tackled the second cycle of Müller poems. The first twelve songs of *Winterreise* appeared in January 1828, not long after Schubert had begun composing the concluding twelve songs. Rather than write a hundred songs or more a year as he did as a teenager, Schubert now composed about a dozen annually, many of which are among his greatest: *Im Frühling*, *Der Wanderer an den Mond*, *Der Winterabend*, and others.

Chamber music continued to exert a special attraction, largely because of Schuppanzigh's strong advocacy. Schubert may have reasoned that quartets and trios, unlike symphonies and operas, seemed to get performed and published. Especially in his chamber music with piano, Schubert pursued a more popular style, just as he had years earlier in the "Trout" Quintet. The reputation of these pieces suffers somewhat in comparison to the late string quartets and the quintet because they tend to be more social and immediately entertaining. In some instances, Schubert also wrote flashy virtuoso pieces, a strategy that did not always prove successful.

While modern commentators often belittle the "Arpeggione" Sonata (D821, written in 1824 for an obscure instrument that was a sort of bowed guitar), and two late violin works – the Rondo in B Minor (D895) and the Fantasy in C (D934) – contemporaries generally held a higher opinion of these works. In 1826, Schubert met a young Bohemian violin virtuoso named Josef Slawjk, for whom he composed the two showpieces. Together with pianist Karl Maria von Bocklet, Slawjk gave a private performance of the Rondo for publisher Domenico Artaria, who released the composition the following year with the title *Rondeau brillant*, Op. 70. Critics commended Schubert's skill in creating something more substantial than the usual trivial entertainment that filled publishers' catalogues and dominated the public concerts of the time. One review of the Rondo declared:

> Although the whole piece is brilliant, it does not owe its existence to mere figurations such as grin at us in a thousand different contortions from so many compositions and are a weariness to the spirit. The spirit of invention has here often beaten its wings mightily indeed and has borne us aloft with it. (SDB 781–82)

Slawjk's première of the Violin Fantasy in January 1828 met with less approbation, but this was due more to his performance than to the merits of the piece itself. Three critics panned the concert, one of them complaining that the Fantasy was too long – longer than a "Viennese is prepared to devote to pleasures of the mind. The hall emptied gradually." Such remarks had consequences. A publisher soon thereafter informed Schubert that he did not want the Fantasy, "for this has been unfavorably criticized in the Leipzig *Allgemeine musikalische Zeitung*" (SDB 716, 767).

Schubert's essays in the virtuoso style, written primarily during his last years, might have been meant to impress audiences with yet another side of his musical personality, even if he could not hope to perform them himself as Paganini and Liszt did so triumphally. Schubert did, however, begin to promote some of his music through public performance. During his final two years, he rather frequently accompanied various singers in presentations of his songs and part-songs. Before 1827, his only documented appearances were conducting the première of his Mass in F in 1814, and as one of four pianists playing an "Italian Overture," transcribed for eight hands, in 1818.

Most importantly, with uncharacteristic assertiveness, Schubert entered into protracted negotiations with prominent foreign publishers in an effort to get a wide variety of music released. Publishers generally sought easy, accessible, marketable trivia, and Schubert's correspondence is filled with requests from them for just such fare.

The Leipzig publisher Probst wanted "not too difficult piano compositions for two or four hands, agreeable and easily comprehensible"; works "which, without sacrificing any of your individuality, are yet not difficult to grasp" (SDB 550, 735). He asked Schubert to send him "very soon some selected trifles for the voice or for four hands," and later inquired if he had "anything easily understandable for piano duet . . . rather like your variations of the miller's song from *Marie* [D908]" (SDB 767, 814). Schubert also satisfied demand with the vocal trios *Der Hochzeitsbraten* and *Die Advocaten* (written years earlier but published in 1827), delightful examples of vocal chamber music without any pretense or deeper worth. He published some Italian songs (D902) and other popular, comic, and refrain songs (D866).

These initiatives are often viewed as stemming simply from financial necessity. As he enjoyed no permanent position and did not want to give lessons, and as there were no rich patrons who regularly supported him, Schubert was constantly having to consider alternative sources of income. And although performance and publication fees therefore surely played a role in his thinking, he also had a more pressing agenda. Schubert was willing to appease publishers and to accept lower sums just so as "to make a start at last." By 1827, he had dealt with most of the major Viennese publishing firms and now wanted to find ways to give his works "greater currency abroad" (SDB 774, 739). Probst wrote praising his songs and piano compositions, which "convince me more and more that it would be easy to disseminate your name throughout the rest of Germany and the North; in this I will gladly lend a hand, considering your talents" (SDB 735). The Mainz firm of B. Schott's Söhne approached him, claiming that it had known of his works during the years when its energies were devoted to publishing Beethoven's last works, the string quartets Schuppanzigh had premiered in Vienna. Schubert offered Schott one of the piano trios, the String Quartets in D Minor and G Major, Four Impromptus (D935), the four-hand F Minor Fantasy (D940), and the Violin Fantasy, as well as various Lieder and partsongs: "This is a list of my finished compositions, excepting three operas, a Mass, and a symphony. These last compositions I mention only in order to make you acquainted with my strivings after the highest in art" (SDB 739). I referred to this letter earlier because at first the comment seems curious: Schubert had written some eight operas, five masses, seven (and a half) symphonies and so much else; yet he willingly acknowledged only fully mature pieces.

Schubert's "strivings after the highest in art" resonate with the larger ambition of his mature years. His negotiations with German publishers reflect a desire for recognition beyond Vienna and the knowledge that publications would provide an impetus for more serious criticism. The sheer number of reviews, as well as their length and import, grew dramatically as Schubert gradually became known as more than just a song and dance composer. In the past, the Viennese press had generally offered strong support and sometimes even called him a genius. Foreign criticism, especially in the influential Leipzig *Allgemeine musikalische Zeitung*, had been more limited in scope and not always as supportive, but that too began to change.

A further point is worth emphasizing again about this criticism: almost every review of Schubert's keyboard and other instrumental music mentions Beethoven. The Leipzig journal did so repeatedly, beginning with its first notice of Schubert in 1820 (SDB 139). Comparisons sometimes worked to Schubert's benefit: the "freedom and originality" of the A Minor Piano Sonata, Op. 42 (D845), can "probably be compared only with the greatest and freest of Beethoven's sonatas. We are indebted for this uncommonly attractive and also significant work to Herr Franz Schubert, who is, we hear, a still quite young artist of and in Vienna" (SDB 512). Reviewing the Sonata in G, Op. 78 (D894), the Leipzig critic proclaimed: "The composer, who has made for himself a numerous following by not a few excellent songs, is capable of doing the same by means of piano pieces." The same review promptly warned Schubert about the dangers of using a unique genius as a model: "Beethoven appears to us to be in a class by himself alone, as it were, especially as he showed himself in his middle and later period, so that in truth he should not by any

Einladung

zu dem Privat Concerte, welches Franz Schubert am 26 März, Abends 7 Uhr im Locale des österreich. Musikvereins unter den Tuchlauben N° 558 zugeben die Ehre haben wird.

Vorkommende Stücke

1. Erster Satz eines neuen Streich. Quartetts, vorgetragen von den Herren Böhm, Holz Weiß und Linke
2. a) Der Kreutzzug von Leitner
   b) Die Sterne von demselben
   c) Der Wanderer a. d. Mond v. Seidl
   d) Fragment aus dem Aeschylus
   Gesänge mit Begleitung des Piano Forte vorgetragen von Herrn Vogl k. k. pensionierten Hofopernsänger
3. Ständchen von Grillparzer, Sopran Solo und Chor vorgetr. von Fräulein Josephine Fröhlich und den Schülerinnen des Conservatoriums
4. Neues Trio für das Piano Forte, Violin und Violoncelle, vorgetragen von den Herren Carl Maria von Boklet, Böhm und Linke
5. Auf dem Strome von Rellstab Gesang mit Begleitung des Horn's und Piano Forte, vorgetragen von den Herren Tietze, und Lewy dem Jüngern.
6. Die Allmacht, von Ladislaus Pyrker, Gesang mit Begleitung des Piano Forte, vorgetragen von Herrn Vogl
7. Schlachtgesang von Klopstock, Doppelchor für Mannenstimmen.

Sämtliche Musikstücke sind von der Composition des Concertgebers

Eintrittskarten zu f 3 W. W. sind in den Kunsthandlungen der Herren Haslinger, Diabelli und Leidesdorf zu haben.

16 The program of Schubert's concert on 26 March 1828, the first anniversary of Beethoven's death.

means be chosen as an absolute model, since anyone who desired to be successful in that master's own line could only be he himself" (SDB 693f). The measuring of Schubert's music by Beethovenian standards began during their lifetimes. Schubert lived with it constantly.

The other essential component in Schubert's quest for wider recognition was distinguished public performances, and in this he sought to expand the exposure afforded by Gesellschaft concerts and Schuppanzigh's subscription series. Although earlier hopes for a "public Schubertiade" had never amounted to anything, in 1828 Schubert and friends arranged an academy for which the Gesellschaft der Musikfreunde provided free use of its facilities at the house Zum roten Igel (Red Hedgehog) in the Tuchlauben. The concert took place on 26 March – a significant date, as it marked the first anniversary of Beethoven's death.

At last, Schubert had the chance to present his newest and best work to the general public and to critics. The programming choices he made are revealing as they show a particular eagerness to showcase instrumental pieces that would display his ability to compose serious compositions. The concert began with the first movement of a "new string quartet," probably his latest one in G Major. The Piano Trio in E-Flat Major, Op. 100 (D929), soon to be his first work published outside Vienna, by Probst in Leipzig, formed the centerpiece. The remainder of the program consisted of Lieder and ambitious partsongs that demonstrated how successfully Schubert had elevated these once lowly genres to more prominent artistic stature. Auf dem Strom is a long song with horn obbligato that sets a poem by Ludwig Rellstab. Ständchen (D920) is one of only three texts that Schubert set by his friend Grillparzer, and it proved to be among his most poignant and affecting partsongs. The evening concluded with the rousing Schlachtlied, a double-chorus setting of a Klopstock poem. Schubert was the pianist for the vocal compositions. In addition to Vogl, who made a rare appearance singing Lieder in public, the distinguished performers of the chamber music were the ones who had premiered Beethoven's own late chamber music. This would have been obvious to many in the audience. (Schuppanzigh did not participate for some reason; he may have been ill.)

"The event was a success in every way and provided Schubert with a considerable sum of money," Sonnleithner recalled (SMF 115), and Bauernfeld noted in his journal, "Enormous applause, good receipts" (SDB 754). Other reports were equally enthusiastic, although Paganini's first appearance in Vienna just three days later diverted the attention of the local press. The Leipzig *Allgemeine musikalische Zeitung* mentioned the concert, in fact likening it to a Beethoven memorial given a few days earlier: "If all these works [by Beethoven], performed to perfection, afforded an indescribable aural treat, the same must be said with hardly less emphasis in praise of that *soirée musicale* which the excellent Schubert held in the very same place on the 26th" (SDB 756).

The popular, critical, and also financial success of Schubert's academy immediately sparked talk of a repeat performance, and he evidently planned to give a similar concert every year (SMF 28). The event exhibits Schubert assuming a new place in Viennese musical life, and the thirty-year-old composer was clearly excited by the prospects. As he proudly reported to the publishers Probst and Schott, "The concert was crammed full . . . I received extraordinary accolades" (SDB 764).

At the time, Schubert was living with Schober's family in the Tuchlauben, right next door to the Gesellschaft der Musikfreunde, where the concert was given. He had moved there the month Beethoven died and remained until shortly before his own death. Schubert made only one trip during this last year and a half, but one that proved especially pleasant. In September 1827, he accompanied Johann Baptist Jenger, a powerful figure in Vienna's musical life and a friend of his, on a three-week holiday in Graz. They were treated royally by the Pachler family. (Marie Pachler was a celebrated pianist, whom Beethoven praised warmly.) He hoped to return the following year, but finances and poor weather foiled his plans. Schubert's lack of funds seems curious, given the money he made from his concert and from the various publishing projects.

With Schober back in Vienna, the reading society was reconstituted; novels by Tieck and Kleist, poems by Heine predominated. We know a considerable amount about the social activities at this time thanks to the diaries of Franz and Fritz von Hartmann, brothers from Linz, who moved to Vienna in the mid 1820s and became part of the circle. As conscientious "pub crawlers," the Hartmanns recorded exactly who appeared at which particular location on a given night, sometimes mentioned what was discussed, and usually noted how long the evening lasted. An invaluable source such as this makes us realize how much information is lost, and how little is in fact known about the daily lives of Schubert and his friends. Franz von Hartmann's entry on 29 June 1828 is the kind that has made some biographers defensive: "To Grinzing [the wine district] with [Karl] Enk and Louis [Hartmann], after having ferreted out Schubert too. All four tipsy, more or less, but Schubert especially. Home at midnight." Some recently published Bauernfeld letters from the summer of 1827 enlarge this picture: "Schubert is living in Dornbach and drinks there . . . he is feeling the inadequacy of our lives." In late summer, Bauernfeld makes the extremely simple and telling remark, "Schubert is drinking less."[4] It was evidently a topic of concern.

The constituency of the pub crawlers was usually entirely male, although women sometimes attended the reading society and often participated in Schubertiades. Schober supposedly told the journalist Ludwig August Frankl that Schubert was in love with the beautiful Auguste Grünwedel and that Schober urged they marry, but that the composer was "firmly convinced no woman could love him," and was upset that "no happiness was granted to him on earth" (SMF 265–66). No other friend mentions their connection in any way, and once again this third-hand report only surfaced forty years after Schubert's death. Schubert did, however, form friendships with an array of impressive women, including actresses Sophie Müller and Katharina Lacsny, Josefine von Koller, the Fröhlich sisters, and Vienna's senior literary lioness, Karoline Pichler. They tended to be highly musical, and Schubert often performed privately for and with them. Yet in general

society Schubert was apparently uncomfortable with women. Anselm
Hüttenbrenner states that his behavior was often "boorish" and "anything but gallant" and that he was physically unkempt (SMF 70).

A few unnamed women of lower social standing are mentioned
in letters and other writings. August Heinrich Hoffmann von
Fallersleben, a minor poet who visited Vienna in the summer of 1827,
wrote in his diary: "From our seat we spied Schubert with his girl
[Mädel]; he came to join us and did not show himself to us again" (SDB
658). As with earlier stories about a possible affair with the chambermaid Pepi Pöckelhofer in Zseliz, the possibility exists that Schubert
pursued casual sexual relations with lower-class women, which
might explain the repeated references to his sensuality.

In the late 1850s, Bauernfeld alluded in a poem to Schubert's particularly strong feelings for an unattainable countess and his involvement with "quite another":

In love was Schubert, one of the young countesses,
For a pupil of his did he smart.
But to quite another he gave himself,
To banish the one from his heart.   (SMF 371)

According to Baron Karl Schönstein, a young noble and fine amateur
Lied singer, whom Schubert had met at the Esterházys' and to whom
Die schöne Müllerin is dedicated, Schubert had a "love affair with a maid
servant [in 1818], which subsequently gave way to a more poetic flame
which sprang up in his heart for the younger daughter of the house,
Countess Caroline. This flame continued to burn until his death.
Caroline had the greatest regard for him and for his talent but did not
return his love; perhaps she had no idea of the degree to which it
existed." In these same 1857 memoirs Schönstein recounts how
Caroline once jokingly chided Schubert for not dedicating any piece to
her, "What is the point? Everything is dedicated to you anyway,"
Schubert allegedly replied (SMF 100). In fact, one outstanding late
work is "composed and dedicated" to Caroline: the magnificent four-
hand keyboard Fantasy in F Minor, Op. 103, which they would likely

have played together. (Caroline possessed a large collection of Schubert's music, including some particularly important manuscripts.)

Schubert taught Caroline during the two summers in Zseliz, as well as in Vienna. A diary entry by Bauernfeld dating from February 1828 is the most substantial evidence of his affection: "Schubert appears seriously in love with Countess E. This pleases me about him. He gives her lessons."[5] Spaun, Schober, Sonnleithner, and others later recalled Schubert's devotion to her, although everyone clearly recognized the futility of the attraction. As Spaun remarked, "[Schubert's] affection for his pupil, the young countess, was an affection which, though hopeless owing to the circumstances, was deep and heartfelt" (SMF 362).

Given the reticence with which Schubert's friends discussed his amours, and the ignorance they professed of any knowledge about them, the repeated and approving references to Caroline seem particularly striking. Casting her as the perfect virgin for an idealized romance, Schubert's friends might have been especially keen to mention Caroline if his physical passions were otherwise realized with prostitutes or in other less orthodox ways. Bauernfeld's reminiscence from 1869 states that Schubert was "head over ears in love" with Caroline and that many of his finest songs from the mid 1820s were "musical self-confessions, bathed in the fire of a true and deep passion, emerged, purified and refined, as genuine works of art of the most perfect kind, from the tender heart of a lover." Bauernfeld immediately proceeds to talk about Schubert's dark side and passions, about his "dual nature," and concludes, "The conflict between unrestrained enjoyment of living and the restless activity of spiritual creation is always exhausting if no balance exists in the soul. Fortunately in our friend's case, an idealized love [*eine ideelle Liebe*] was at work, mediating, reconciling, compensating, and Countess Caroline may be looked upon as his visible, beneficent muse, as the Leonore of this musical Tasso" (SMF 233–34). Indeed, as we have seen, Schwind depicted Caroline as artistic muse when he placed her portrait so prominently in the Spaun Schubertiade illustration. Schubert's "hopeless" devotion to the chaste Caroline mirrors, in a way, his earlier relationship with the young Therese Grob; here, too, we find a connection between the unattainable object of Schubert's supposed affection and his music. Grob, I have suggested, was an early inspiration and the first significant interpreter of his music. Caroline was the untouched and untouchable star from a better world for whom he wrote his greatest piano duets, and perhaps other works. These two musical muses, some unnamed lower-class chambermaids or tavern girls, and passing infatuations with musical friends such as Müller or Koller with whom Schubert may have been infatuated, are the only women connected with Schubert in any romantic way.[6]

Although I think there has been considerable exaggeration of the homoerotic nature (rather than the homosocial) of the entire circle, it seems undeniable that Schubert's male friends, some of whom may have been homosexual or bisexual, were the ones he cared about over the longest period, the ones with whom he spent the greatest amount of time, and the ones with whom he explored his art most deeply. The exact nature of these relationships, however, remains elusive. The extremely candid and gushing professions of love, warmth, and tenderness found in letters among these male friends are striking today, but were not so unusual at the time.[7] The anachronism of calling Schubert a "gay composer" seems to indicate a lack of awareness, on the part of those who do so, of the complexity of the issues involved. The nature of same-sex love at a time and place in which neither the word "homosexual" nor "gay" existed and in which the activities, attitudes, and behavior the category came to denote were often likely quite different from today, is highly problematic to establish. To project views of contemporary culture back onto Biedermeier Vienna seriously distorts the realities of Schubert's life and world. And yet the repeated allusions to Schubert's hedonism, the lack of any satisfactorily documented intimate relationship with a woman, and his overwhelming attachment to and living arrangements with male friends must not be ignored.

The conventional three phases of an artist's career – analogous in some ways to the life stages of youth, maturity, and old age – usually culminate in a final period that is often characterized by a distinctive "late style," producing works of a valedictory and idiosyncratic nature. Bach partly withdrew into esoteric realms of counterpoint, Mozart's late Masonic interests hint at another world, and Liszt's ultimate renunciation of technical bravura in his lean piano works points toward impressionism. Beethoven's late style reveals an unprecedented interiority quite different from the "heroic" affirmations of his middle period. Critics at the time acknowledged that Beethoven worked through personal issues in his pieces, that his music was somehow autobiographical. While commentators began delineating the phases of Beethoven's career during his lifetime, Schubert's oeuvre has proved more resistant to such positioning. Indeed, for one who died so young, talk of a beginning, middle, and end may seem even inappropriate. "Lateness" suggests a summation, a reflective recapitulation generally associated with old age.

What helps us recognize "late Schubert"? Not only distinctive musical features, but also, perhaps, an attitude that informed his aesthetic approach. During his last years Schubert was variously inspired, frustrated, intimidated, and motivated by thoughts of his own mortality and of Beethoven. While his frequent use of Beethoven's works as compositional models – the borrowing of themes and imitation of procedures – is well documented, the revered composer's example went much further, affecting Schubert's notions about the very function and status of the art of music. Beethoven showed him that music could go beyond the beautiful, into the sublime.

Suffering, struggle, and heroism in the face of adversity are often associated with Beethoven, but allusions to Schubert's trials also occur frequently in his friends' letters and reminiscences. When Schwind heard of Schubert's death he wrote to Schober that their friend was now "done with his sorrows. The more I realize now what he was like, the

17 Portrait by an unknown artist of Schubert from the late 1820s.

more I see what he has suffered" (SDB 829). Rather dramatically, some
even suggested that *Winterreise* hastened Schubert's end. Spaun writes
"how deeply his creations affected him [and how] they were conceived
in suffering . . . There is no doubt in my mind that the state of excitement
in which he composed his most beautiful songs, and especially his
Winterreise, contributed to his early death" (SMF 139).

Although the musical manifestations of such emotional states may be more explicit in late Beethoven, stunning moments in Schubert's late works hint at some sort of personal testimony: the wrenching final dissonances of the F Minor Fantasy, the devastating interpolated silences in the last movement of the A Major Piano Sonata, or the otherworldly trills of the B-flat Major Sonata. Late Schubert also offers ebullient movements and passages of consoling lyrical serenity. Disturbing violence increasingly intrudes within slow movements of otherwise incredible beauty, and Schubert will often slip from one place – a particular state of mind – to a totally unexpected and foreign location without any kind of transition. (This latter procedure usually involves extraordinary harmonic daring.) His incorporation of his own songs into instrumental works; self-quotations and subtle allusions to other composers (which even now continue to be discovered); connections among movements and between separate works – all these features seem to carry meaning and to invite interpretation.

Many of Schubert's last songs inhabit a different world from his first masterpieces written fourteen years earlier. They often juxtapose hopeless fatalism with blissful serenity. Although the pairing was a publisher's and not Schubert's own, the conclusion of *Schwanengesang* could not be more contradictory: *Der Doppelgänger* looks directly into the abyss, while *Die Taubenpost* soars upward on wings of song. Mayrhofer remarked the changes in musical style between *Die schöne Müllerin* and *Winterreise*:

> [*Die schöne Müllerin*] opens with a joyous song of roaming, the mill songs depict love in its awakening, its deceptions and hopes, its delights and sorrows . . . Not so with *Winterreise*, the very choice of which shows how much more serious the composer had become. He had been long and seriously ill, had gone through shattering experiences, and life for him had shed its rosy color; winter had come for him. (SMF 15)

Schubert's late music may thus follow Beethoven's model more in aesthetic intent than in explicit musical design. Schubert reveals a new seriousness, subjectivity, and rigorous self-examination that go well beyond the pleasure principle of cozy Schubertiades. The integrity he attained suggests that he no longer wrote music solely for the delight of companions, the profit of publishers, or the entertainment of the public. At his best, he was now writing essentially for himself – and for the future. Some friends found *Winterreise* gloomy, but Spaun reports that to such criticism Schubert responded, "I like these songs more than all the others, and you will come to like them too" (SMF 138).

The late Lieder provide eloquent testimony that, far from abandoning the genres by which he had formed his earlier reputation, Schubert now could use them to explore darker realms. Not that he arrogantly turned his back on his own earlier works, his audience, or his friends. He did, however, think more about his place in musical history. As with Beethoven's then misunderstood last works, many of Schubert's late compositions address posterity. The idea of writing for the future may strike us as a later Romantic one, inappropriate to apply either to Beethoven or to Schubert, and yet the evidence indicates that later generations were indeed on both composers' minds and that this concern constituted a profound change in musical culture. Charges that Beethoven was detached from contemporary audiences were mounted during his last decade, when the perceived strangeness of his new music could be attributed to his eccentricities and deafness. Told that the "quartet which Schuppanzigh played yesterday did not please," Beethoven replied, "It will please them someday." Beethoven made many such comments.

To be sure, Beethoven and Schubert often composed for financial reasons (even Beethoven's late quartets were commissioned), but they also largely wrote what they pleased – Beethoven with the knowledge that anything he produced would be published and performed, Schubert with the hope that the same would be true someday for him. Neither the church, nor the aristocracy, nor other cultural institutions any longer solely guided the highest artistic production. While the public continued to favor the familiar triumphs of Beethoven's middle period, Schubert followed the aesthetic example of his late works, especially of the quartets he encountered through Schuppanzigh. Musicologists have understandably concentrated on the musical influence of specific middle-period works that Schubert used as models, but the deeper attraction of Beethoven's music is not always so clear. Even if Schubert did not live long enough to assimilate fully the musical qualities of Beethoven's late works, he could still be deeply affected by the compositional direction in which they pointed and the artistic credo they embodied. Beethoven's increasing determination to pursue his own course, lead where it may, certainly helped to strengthen Schubert's own convictions.

As early as 1812, Schubert had written an isolated sonata movement for piano trio (D28), and near the end he returned to this popular instrumental combination, perhaps at the suggestion of Beethoven's musicians – Schuppanzigh, Bocklet, and cellist Josef Linke. As the manuscript for the Trio in B-flat, Op. 99 (D898) is lost, its date of composition remains a mystery, although it seems clearly to be the earlier of the two late trios. The Trio in E-flat, Op. 100 (D929), was begun in November 1827 shortly after the six-month anniversary of Beethoven's death, which was commemorated by another Grillparzer oration. The trio was published the month of Schubert's death, exactly one year later.

Schubert chose this work to be the centerpiece of his academy, and I believe he did so for reasons that demonstrate the overwhelming importance that Beethoven's death held for him. Like the older composer's mature piano trios, the E-flat Trio is in four movements – fast, slow, scherzo, and lengthy finale. Schubert explores the cyclical structure of Beethoven's Fifth Symphony, in which motives connect movements and music from an earlier movement is incorporated into a later one. The trio's second movement not only imitates Beethoven, but also honors him. Schubert used the *Marcia funebre* of the *Eroica* as a hidden reference. Beethoven had written that symphony "in memory of a great man" and Schubert here mourns the loss of his own musical hero. The beautiful C-minor cello melody atop a processional piano accompaniment in the first measures projects a similar melodic gesture to the beginning of the second movement of the *Eroica*. The openings also share the same tonality and the distinctive dotted sixteenth, thirty-second note rhythm.

While previous commentators have called Schubert's movement a funeral march, and a few have noticed the tonal, melodic, and structural similarities to Beethoven's symphony, the greater meaning has remained secret. Leopold von Sonnleithner reported that Schubert made use of a Swedish melody in this movement, and it is usually assumed that he was referring to the haunting opening melody. In fact a Swedish song, *Se solen sjunker* ("See, the sun is setting") only enters later in the movement, with a distinctive motive of a falling octave. The words of the song at that moment further reveal the movement's message: "Farewell! Farewell!"

Larger structural procedures over the course of the movement reinforce the conviction that Schubert had the *Eroica* in his mind. Just as both movements begin similarly, they end the same way; Schubert even includes a literal quotation of a flute and violin passage from Beethoven's own concluding measures in the trio's ending, immediately before the closing falling octave motive intones a final farewell. Moreover, Schubert later "remembers" the elegiac cello melody three times in the final movement. His most ambitious chamber composition to date, and the one he valued most highly, is a *Tombeau de Beethoven*.[8]

Schubert may not have divulged this "secret program" to anyone, but it shows another important side of the composer and of his late concerns. We must remember that the trio was performed by Beethoven's favorite musicians at the 26 March 1828 concert, held on the first anniversary of Beethoven's death. For this same event, Schubert specially composed *Auf dem Strom*, which musicologist Rufus Hallmark discovered also makes reference to the funeral march of the *Eroica*.[9] While Schubert's self-quotations in instrumental compositions are well known, these two coded tributes to Beethoven suggest that he used the device more often than previously thought, that he did not limit the raw material to his own songs, and that such allusions can offer hermeneutic keys to certain works. Most impressively, Schubert composed an homage inspired by Beethoven, but one that does not slavishly copy him. Even when Schubert drew upon Beethoven in his late works, he did so in his own distinctive voice.

In retrospect, 1828 featured some uncanny premonitions of Schubert's death. Bauernfeld prophesied in his annual New Year's ode:

> The magic of speech, the source of songs
> They too will dry up, divine as they are;
> No longer will songs pour forth in a flood,
> For the singer too will be carried away:
> The waters flow back to the sea,
> The singer of songs to the source of the songs.   (SDB 703)

And Schubert, for the first time, as far as we know, signed off a letter to Anselm Hüttenbrenner thus: "I remain, your faithful friend until death – Frz. Schubert." Yet however significant such matters may appear in retrospect, and however valedictory so many of his extraordinary final compositions, there does not seem to have been any special reason for Schubert to feel that his end was fast approaching. Aside from passing complaints about his "usual headaches" and his inability to appear at various times, such as a party in October 1827 ("I am ill, and in a way which totally unfits me for such a gathering"), there is little indication of a steady decline (SDB 679,681). By all accounts, Schubert's death took friends by surprise.

During his serious illness in 1823 and 1824, Schubert had clearly despaired about his future and of his chances for leading a full and conventional life. There is reason to believe that he underwent mercury treatment that may have proved beneficial. (Recent studies note that the photographs of Schubert's skull, taken in 1863 when his body was exhumed, do not show the skeletal alterations typical of advanced, untreated syphilis.) Although his health was undoubtedly damaged, he may not have been living under a death sentence like that of some cancer or AIDS sufferers today.

In 1827 and 1828 we continue to encounter the hopeful plans Schubert had outlined to Kupelwieser in 1824, while also noting a greater sense of urgency. In his dealings with Probst and Schott, he requested they proceed "as soon as possible." The correspondence concerning the E-flat Piano Trio comes close to desperation. Schubert accepted a low fee but insisted on "the speediest possible publication." After several delays Probst solicited the opus number and dedication, to which Schubert responded: "The opus number of the Trio is 100. I request that the edition should be faultless and I look forward to it longingly. This work is to be dedicated to nobody, save those who find pleasure in it. This is the most profitable dedication." When the publication still had not arrived two months later, Schubert asked yet again: "I beg to inquire when the Trio is to appear at last. Can it be that you do not know the opus number yet? It is Op. 100. I await its appearance with longing" (SDB 774 ,796, 810). He probably never saw the edition, issued the month he died.

Schubert's unprecedented determination in arranging performances and publications did not slow the pace of his composing, which, in fact, accelerated. Even though we now know that the "Great" C Major Symphony was written several years earlier, the quantity of pieces from his last year – and their range – still astonishes. Yet we should note that not all was gold, or even silver, and that lesser compositions also date from these last years. Social music still stood the greatest chance of everyday consumption and ready publication, and Schubert aimed for popular success through virtuoso pieces, such as the violin works mentioned earlier, through partsongs, dances, and so forth. He wrote virtuoso displays including the rather trivial Variations for Flute and Piano (D802) in 1824, based on the song *Trockne Blumen* from *Die schöne Müllerin*, and later the more charming *Der Hirt auf dem Felsen* (D965), a hybrid Lied-cantata to a text by Müller and Helmina von Chézy that includes a clarinet obbligato.

Schubert also returned to composing sacred music. In 1826 he revised part of his Mass in A-flat and in the final summer wrote another Mass in E-flat (D950). The Leipzig *Allgemeine musikalische Zeitung* criticized its "dark style," which lent it the feeling of a Requiem, and indeed the final Agnus Dei shares the same four-note ostinato bass as *Der Doppelgänger*. A curiosity from the same time is a setting of Psalm 92 (D953). Although he had earlier set Psalms 13 and 23 in Moses Mendelssohn's German translation, this late *a cappella* setting uses the Hebrew text and was written for Salomon Sulzer (1804–90), the remarkable young cantor of the new Seiten-stettengasse Temple. And in Schubert's very last month he composed a handful of smaller religious works. Could some employment prospect have prompted this rather unexpected activity?

Three stunning late works for piano duet – the Fantasy in F Minor (D940), the Allegro in A Minor (D947, "Lebensstürme"), and the Rondo in A (D951) – serve as additional proof of Schubert's quest to transcend the confines of the salon. Schubert's music for piano duet is among not only his greatest but also his most original. Such innovations may explain why his attraction to the medium continued even after his energies shifted increasingly to large-scale instrumental works. Indeed, the audacious harmonic and structural adventures in his finest keyboard duets may have pointed the way to orchestral projects that he did not live to realize. (The "Grand Duo" some years earlier had served a comparable preparatory purpose with regard to large-scale form.) In any case, the late piano duets exquisitely merge Schubert's lyrical gifts with daring formal structures.

The F Minor Fantasy represents a refinement of the "Wanderer" Fantasy, abandoning the explosive bravura of the earlier work's opening in favor of an elegiac theme that is unforgettable upon first hearing. Before the Romantic period the designation "fantasy" usually implied an improvisatory style and structural freedom. But in his mature fantasies Schubert, following Beethoven, expands traditional formal designs to create tightly constructed works. He boldly merges four movements into one, an innovation that would strongly influence Liszt's compositions. At the same time, this fantasy, like the "Wanderer," may be considered a sonata form, with the Largo and Scherzo serving as development. The middle movements prove Schubert to be a master of transition; they flow seamlessly, almost inevitably, from what precedes. All sections are subtly related through the recurring appearance of dotted rhythms, the prevalence of the interval of the rising fourth, the characteristic Schubertian shifts between major and minor, and the prominence of ornamental trills. The coherence of Schubert's progressive structure is unmistakable when the haunting theme that opens the work reappears at the opening of the fourth "movement," both acting as a recapitulation and leading to a monumental, Beethovenian, fugue. The wondrous theme appears once more, as a coda, a final gesture of intimacy and longing before the extraordinary dissonances of the closing measures.

The late solo piano music includes both smaller works and the last three sonatas. Schubert was fairly successful in publishing keyboard works, especially short Impromptus (D899, D935) and Moments Musicaux (D780) that helped to establish the Romantic miniature already being explored by the Bohemian composers Václav Tomášek and Jan Voříšek. Schubert wrote his two sets of Impromptus, each containing four separate pieces, in late 1827. Although the title suggests an unpremeditated, perhaps even improvisatory piece, Schubert's Impromptus are usually clearly structured. Schumann believed that the second set actually contained parts of a sonata in disguise: "every page . . . breathes 'Franz Schubert.'"[10] In 1828 Schubert composed three more separate pieces, the *Drei Klavierstücke* (D946), which have been considered a set ever since Brahms anonymously edited and published them in 1868.

Schubert dated the last three piano sonatas "September," although surviving drafts suggest a longer genesis over the summer months. He also labeled them as a set and intended a dedication to Hummel. Despite fascinating interrelations among them, each sonata projects a distinctive character. The C Minor (D958) is one of the most explicitly Beethovenian works Schubert ever wrote and is especially close to some of the earlier composer's works in the same key. The A Major Sonata (D959) uses Beethoven's Sonata Op. 31, No. 1 as a structural model for the last movement, even as Schubert recycles his own melody (a theme he had used for the slow movement of his A Minor Sonata [D537]) and makes the mood all his own. The last Sonata in B-flat Major (D960) enjoys the highest critical esteem and, like the String Quintet in C, synthesizes many of Schubert's stylistic features. Some of the extraordinary qualities of the quintet, written around the same time as the sonatas, were discussed earlier. Unlike Mozart's string quintets, which use two violas, Schubert employs an additional cello, lending the work a darker tone and allowing one cello to sing while the other provides harmonic support. The quintet exhibits the ultimate refinement of much that is valued in Schubert – the melting lyricism, unexpected modulations, shifts to unexpected places, eclectic mixture of moods, and the calm beauty of a slow movement that is interrupted by terrifying anguish.

The final songs show not only how Schubert "invented" the Romantic Lied, but also how he anticipated the future of the genre. As savvy publishers have long known, a composer's last work can be effectively marketed. The publisher Tobias Haslinger, a friend of Beethoven's, began his business association with Schubert relatively late. He acquired Schubert's last songs and sonatas from Ferdinand immediately after the composer's death, announcing in the *Wiener Zeitung* the upcoming publication of "fourteen as yet wholly unknown songs with piano accompaniment (composed in August 1828) and three piano sonatas (composed in September 1828)" (SDB 844). A few months later the songs were advertised under the title *Schwanengesang* as Schubert's "last work" – the "last blossoms of his noble strength." A special subscription edition featured an engraving of a swan swimming at sunset and named 158 subscribers to the 180 copies ordered. This list would also "appear as a survey of Schubert's admirers and friends, indeed in a way represent a list of the mourners' names."[11] In a memorial essay about him, Spaun said the "fourteen quite new songs" were intended by Schubert to be "dedicated to his friends," including *Die Taubenpost*, "which was his last" (SDB 875).

For these songs Schubert looked to three contemporary poets. Haslinger's grouping creates a different kind of "song cycle" without the obvious narrative cohesion of the earlier Müller cycles. Schubert did not intend the sentimental title, or the inclusion of *Die Taubenpost*, but he apparently wanted the seven Rellstab and six Heine settings to be grouped according to the poet. Ludwig Rellstab (1799–1860), a music critic who lived in Berlin, visited Vienna in 1825, and met Beethoven, with whom he discussed the possibility of collaborating on an opera. He sent Beethoven handwritten copies of unpublished poems, which Schindler allegedly handed over to Schubert after Beethoven's death. According to Rellstab, Schindler returned the poems to him with pencil marks in Beethoven's hand indicating "the ones he liked best and the ones he had given Schubert to compose at that time, because he himself felt too unwell" (SMF 303).

Schubert set only six poems by his exact contemporary, the outstanding poet and critic Heinrich Heine (1797–1856). All six are drawn from the untitled poems in Heine's collection *Die Heimkehr*, written in 1823–24 and published two years later in the first part of his *Reisebilder*. Haslinger added *Die Taubenpost*, set to a poem by the young Viennese writer Johann Gabriel Seidl (1804–75), perhaps because thirteen songs would have been too unlucky a number for this posthumous collection or more simply because the song was apparently Schubert's swan-song. (The other candidate is *Der Hirt auf dem Felsen*.) A recently discovered letter reveals that a Schubertiade was held at Spaun's home on 23 December 1828, just over a month after Schubert's death, at which "Vogl sang Schubert's final, as-yet-unknown compositions from the months of September and October, including the last song composed before his death, 'Die Brieftaube' [*Die Taubenpost*], one of the most delightful of his songs, and another, *Der Doppelgänger*, one of the blackest night-pieces among his songs."[12]

In his final Lieder, Schubert reflects one last time on many beloved themes that reappear throughout his career, such as love and nature, the image of the wanderer, and explorations of death. Some songs feature objects that repeatedly attracted him, for instance babbling brooks, strumming guitars, and galloping horses. In *Liebesbotschaft* the brook is once again a lover's confidant, a "messenger of love" that briefly reappears in *Frühlingssehnsucht*. *Abschied* marks Schubert's farewell to the perpetual-motion galloping songs made famous with *Erlkönig*. He revisits standard structures in some songs, while he pushes formal limits in others. None of the songs in *Schwanengesang* is strictly strophic – the same music for each verse – as were so many songs from Schubert's early years (and even eight of the twenty in *Die schöne Müllerin*), although he still experiments with modifications of strophic form. *Kriegers Ahnung* shows how far he had developed since his early narrative songs, which often verge on operatic *scenas*. The four sections in this setting, in differing keys, tempos, and meters, trace a progression of meditations – first dark, then more hopeful, and finally resigned.

Not everything is farewell: the Heine songs in particular look both forward and back. The declamatory style of Schubert's earliest songs is masterfully refined to an economy that presages late Romanticism. Schubert's declamation achieves what Wagner would later formulate as the ideal of musical art: "endless melody" in which every note is expressive, eloquent, and meaningful. *Der Doppelgänger*, the thirteenth song, is a frightening work whose opening piano passacaglia looks back to Bach's C-sharp Minor Fugue from the first book of the *Well-Tempered Clavier*, as well as to Schubert's own overture to *Fierabras* and the Agnus Dei of the E-flat Mass. This uncanny song, which some consider Schubert's greatest, points to the rest of the nineteenth century and beyond, not only in its pioneering musical style but, even more remarkably, in its existential mood. One is reminded of the prophetic comment Schubert allegedly made to Anschütz: "Sometimes it seems to me I no longer belonged to this world" (SMF 224). The lofty place the Heine Lieder now hold in critical esteem testifies to the profound change in how we have come to understand Schubert, both the man and the composer. The musical as well as psychological innovations of these songs are analogous to those in Beethoven's late quartets. It seems appropriate that Schubert's latest breakthrough came in the realm of song.

18   Sketch page of Schubert's unfinished Symphony in D (D936a), which may be
the last music he wrote. Counterpoint exercises begin the page.

Although *Der Hirt auf dem Felsen* and *Die Taubenpost* appear to be
Schubert's last two songs, they may not be the last notes he set
to paper. Fascinating sketches for a three-movement "Tenth"
Symphony (D936a), written on a type of paper Schubert used in his
last months, include a haunting second movement, an Andante,
which contains marginalia in Schubert's hand connected with the
counterpoint lesson he took with the noted theorist Simon Sechter
(1788–1867) on 4 November, just two weeks before his death. This
final unfinished symphony – which really is Schubert's Unfinished
Symphony – looks far into the future and shows Schubert's late
interest in counterpoint. Near his end, Schubert, like Beethoven,
looked to the past, specifically to Handel, for inspiration. (It is even
possible that Haslinger lent him volumes from Arnold's new
English edition of Handel's works that were part of Beethoven's
estate.) According to Sonnleithner, Schubert acquired scores of
Handel oratorios and said, "Now for the first time I see what I lack;

but I will study hard with Sechter so that I can make good the omission" (SMF 114; cf. 177, 180, 255). Schubert's *Mirjams Siegesgesang* is testimony to this interest. When this late work was first performed two months after his death, a critic perceptively observed that Schubert was able to "fuse powerful seriousness of Handel with the fiery passion of Beethoven."[13]

At the beginning of November, Schubert began his counterpoint lessons, but illness prevented more than a single meeting. Some exercises survive with Sechter's corrections. Schubert's supposed "need" (rather than wish) to take lessons at the very time he was writing his greatest music has baffled some commentators and spurred on detractors who cite Schubert's self-initiated study as proof that he could not handle counterpoint or large structures. The impetus may simply have been intellectual curiosity born of the encounter with Handel's music, as well as the chance to discuss counterpoint with an expert. The sole lesson with Sechter later received far more attention than was warranted; both Leopold von Sonnleithner and Mayrhofer mention the instruction in their 1829 memorials to Schubert.

Unable to leave the city during the summer of 1828 or to travel to Graz as he had hoped, Schubert continued to live at Schober's. Perhaps his doctor suggested that he move to safer ground and fresher air, for at the beginning of September he went to stay with Ferdinand. During Schubert's last ten weeks, his brother cared for him in his apartment, located on what is today Kettenbrückengasse in the district of Wieden. The typical multifamily house had been erected only the year before, and the damp surroundings worsened matters (SMF 37, 196). Schubert's last documented excursion suggests a preoccupation with death, greatness, and thoughts of posterity as his own end drew near. In early October, he joined Ferdinand and some friends for a three-day walking tour of Lower Austria to visit Joseph Haydn's grave in Eisenstadt in Burgenland. Surely such a long trip – some thirty-five miles each way – would not only have been inadvisable, but also impossible, for a seriously ill man. This excursion, the fact that he left his belongings at Schober's, where he planned to return, and his continued compositional pace all suggest that Schubert was trying to build his strength and health, not that he was hurtling toward death.

On the last day of the month Schubert went to dinner at the inn Zum roten Kreuz, not far from where he was born, but found the fish served repelling. The next day he is said to have heard a Requiem written by Ferdinand at a church in the Hernals suburb; later in the week he took his lesson with Sechter. Schubert wrote what was probably his last letter a week before he died to Schober:

> I am ill. I have had nothing to eat or drink for eleven days now, and can only wander feebly and uncertainly between armchair and bed. [My doctor] Rinna is treating me. If I take any food I cannot retain it at all.
>
> So please be so good as to come to my aid in this desperate condition with something to read. I have read Cooper's *Last of the Mohicans*, *The Spy*, *The Pilot*, and *The Pioneers*. If by chance you have anything else of his, I beg you to leave it for me at the coffee-house with Frau von Bogner. My brother, who is conscientiousness itself, will bring it over to me without fail. Or indeed anything else. Your Friend, Schubert. (SDB 820)

What caused the final illness? The death register states that Schubert succumbed to "nervous fever," which was then a fairly generic label (his mother died of the same cause). As mentioned, there does not appear to have been any precipitous decline in his health, although he sometimes felt unfit to venture out and complained of headaches. One obituary mentioned that "except for frequent pains in his head, Schubert, with his robust physique, enjoyed lasting good health" (SMF 10). There have been various studies of Schubert's death, and the diagnosis is not settled. Tertiary syphilis is one possibility, or complications from that condition (undoubtedly his immune system was weakened by the disease), or typhoid fever, or something else.[14]

At the end, it appears, Schubert's thoughts again turned to Beethoven. Karl Holz, who had played Schubert's chamber music in concert with Schuppanzigh, allegedly arranged a private bedside performance of Beethoven's String Quartet in C-sharp Minor, Op. 131, at Schubert's request. According to Holz, as reported later by music historian Ludwig Nohl, "Schubert was sent into such transports of delight and enthusiasm and was so overcome that [we] all feared for him . . . The quartet was the last music he heard. The king of harmony had sent the king of song a friendly bidding to the crossing!" (SMF 299).

Spaun states that Schubert spent his last days correcting the proofs for the second part of *Winterreise*. The composer's death was unexpected, for when Spaun visited, Schubert was

> ill in bed, though his condition did not seem to me at all serious . . .
> he was cared for most affectionately by a charming thirteen-year-old
> sister . . . I left him without any anxiety at all, and it came as a
> thunderbolt when, a few days later, I heard of his death. Poor
> Schubert, so young and at the start of a brilliant career! What a wealth
> of untapped treasures his death has robbed us of! (SMF 139)

Bauernfeld later remembered the end. He visited on 17 November and found Schubert

> very weak, but quiet and not without hope of recovery; he also
> expressed the lively wish to receive another new opera libretto.
> However, on the same evening he became more violently delirious,
> having been but intermittently and feebly stricken before, and
> scarcely grew more lucid again; his illness had passed into a virulent
> attack of typhoid fever, and on November 19th at 3 o'clock in the
> afternoon, he passed away. (SMF 33)

8 Immortal Schubert: "Composing invisibly"

If Schubert's contemporaries justly gazed in astonishment at his creative power, what indeed must we, who come after him, say, as we incessantly discover new works of his? For thirty years the master has been dead, and in spite of this it seems as if he goes on composing invisibly – it is impossible to keep up with him.

Eduard Hanslick, 1862

At dawn two days after his brother's death, Ferdinand wrote to their father, "Very many people have expressed the wish that the body of our good Franz be buried in the sacred ground of Währing Cemetery. I too am among them, because I believe Franz himself made this request." In a delirium before he died, Schubert did not know where he was and cried out, "This is not where Beethoven lies." For Ferdinand this could be nothing more than "an indication of his last wish to be buried beside Beethoven, whom he so greatly revered." Ferdinand informed his father that he had already explored the expenses involved, which although very high were "surely very little for Franz!" He offered to pay more than half the cost himself (SDB 825).

The composer's final wish, at least according to Ferdinand's interpretation, was granted. Schubert was buried later that day, without much pomp and circumstance, following a well-attended funeral, but one that hardly attracted tens of thousands of mourners, as Beethoven's had just twenty months earlier. Schubert's *Pax vobiscum*

(D551), fitted with new words by Schober, was played at the church. Schubert was buried in the new Währing Cemetery, and his grave placed as close to Beethoven's as possible, just three away. A memorial service the next month featured a Mass by Anselm Hüttenbrenner (SMF 121, 190), and plans were announced to raise money for a fitting funeral monument. On 30 January 1829, the eve of Schubert's thirty-second birthday, Anna Fröhlich, Vogl, Böhm, Linke, and other musician friends presented a memorial concert in the hall where Schubert's own academy of 26 March 1828 had taken place (SDB 851); they offered a quite similar program, presenting it again six weeks later.

These events succeeded in raising enough money for the tombstone, which Schober reportedly helped to design and which was executed by the architect Ludwig Förster (SMF 89). A bust of Schubert sculpted by Josef Alois Dialer was placed in a niche over an epitaph written by Grillparzer. It fell to the poet as well to announce the grave site:

> This is to inform all friends and admirers of Schubert, especially those who have shown their feelings for him by their contributions to his monument, that this has now been finished by craftsman's hands and decorated with a cast iron bust in the likeness of the departed.
> (SDB 907)

The Vienna *Allgemeiner musikalischer Anzeiger* stated that the "tombstone is simple – as simple as [Schubert's] songs; but it conceals a profound soul, as they do" (SDB 907).

Grillparzer had attended many Schubertiades, and other occasions had brought him together with Schubert fairly frequently, but the two were apparently not intimate friends, and Schubert set only a few of his poems. Just as Grillparzer's eminent literary stature had made him the obvious choice to compose the funeral oration for Beethoven (they too had been acquaintances), it seemed appropriate that he compose a fitting epitaph for Schubert. He sketched five possibilities, some quite tentative, which reveal Schubert's stature at the time by

19 Contemporary photograph of Schubert's First Grave in Währing Cemetery with a bust by Franz Dialer and epitaph by Franz Grillparzer.

concentrating on his songs (SDB 899). The one ultimately chosen proved controversial: THE ART OF MUSIC HERE ENTOMBED A RICH POSSESSION, BUT EVEN FAR FAIRER HOPES. Although years later Robert Schumann would attack the sentiment of the epitaph, arguing that is was "pointless to guess at what more [Schubert] might have achieved,"[1] other Schubertians echoed and applauded Grillparzer. Franz Lachner commended the "absolute truth of the epitaph written for him by our mutual friend Grillparzer" (SMF 290).

Perhaps the epitaph is more usefully viewed not as a lament over unrealized hopes or as sorrow at such an early demise, but rather as an indication of how little was known about Schubert's accomplishment at the time of his death. The true scope of what he had done eluded even his most sympathetic admirers. Spaun considered Schubert a great Lied composer, but expressed private doubts about his instrumental, choral, and dramatic works. He sidestepped the issue in his 1829 memorial: "Whether Schubert's larger works are also of the first quality, the future will show" (SMF 25; cf. 30, 140, 355). Many obituaries, tributes, and memorial poems referred to Schubert's untimely passing; the allusions would continue for decades. The aura of incompleteness that surrounds Schubert's fame – and Mozart's – has less to do with the actual amount of music they created than with the abbreviated period in which they worked. Small wonder that these two composers in particular are so often viewed as "naturals"; they had so little time to work their miracles.

The reality of Schubert's early death carries tremendous weight. In this respect his most famous and popular instrumental work, the "Unfinished" Symphony, proves instructive on two counts. First, its première took place well over forty years after its composition. This delayed unveiling powerfully underscores how relatively obscure so much of Schubert's music was even as late as the 1860s and how his reputation therefore continually had to be reevaluated. Second, as I mentioned in chapter 1, the nickname epitomizes the unfinished quality of Schubert's life and art, and serves as a fitting metaphor, a recurring reminder of unfulfilled promise – the very theme sounded by Grillparzer's epitaph. Although the symphony does not have an explicit "program," as so many nineteenth-century composers would apply to their pieces, the nickname subtly and seductively serves as an unintended programmatic crutch.

The symbolic significance of the "Unfinished" Symphony and the disagreements concerning the epitaph bring to light two related issues: the actual course of Schubert's posthumous reception and the perpetual fantasies about "treasures" he did not live long enough to create. If we look at the opportunities that emerged during Schubert's final years and at the direction that his reception took during the decades following his death, we can speculate fairly responsibly about how his professional career might have flourished had he lived longer. At the time he died, Schubert was arguably on the brink of real fame. Beethoven's passing had opened a space, both literal and figurative. As Schott informed Schubert in 1828, the publishing firm was approaching him only after having completed the release of the late Beethoven quartets. Schuppanzigh and other leading Viennese musicians wanted – and needed – new music to perform. And Schubert must have been responding on some level to Grillparzer's challenge voiced at Beethoven's funeral, concerning the next great composer; as we have seen, he displayed uncharacteristic resolve in his efforts to achieve a new stature. At the end of his life, Schubert was not only writing his greatest music, but also finally beginning to be recognized for some of his breakthroughs. This ascendance surely would have accelerated, especially given the likely support of the next generation of Romantics – Schumann, Liszt, Mendelssohn, and Brahms – who in any event did much to promote Schubert's posthumous cause.

Posterity, however, has focused on the more complicated and conjectural question of what further masterpieces Schubert might have created. Some evidence is tangible. The "Tenth" Symphony (D936a) and the Bauernfeld opera, *Der Graf von Gleichen* (D918), were both far enough along to suggest new directions in these public genres. The last Lieder, partsongs, and four-hand music prove that Schubert, far from abandoning domestic genres, was in fact transcending them – *Hausmusik* for posterity. And the late 1828 keyboard and chamber works – the piano sonatas and string quintet – reveal that the "heavenly length" of Schubert's most ambitious instrumental compositions entailed innovative narrative strategies and manipulations of a listener's feeling of time that are quite different from those of Beethoven. Yet where this all might ultimately have led it is pure fantasy to contemplate. The question of Schubert's unfulfilled promise also fascinates because, it seems, he could not be silenced by death, but rather continued to compose beyond the grave.

"Schubert is dead, and with him all that we had of the brightest and fairest" (SDB 847). Schwind was studying art in Munich when his friend died; he poured out his feelings in a letter to Schober. The news had shocked everyone. Bauernfeld wrote in his diary: "Yesterday afternoon Schubert died. On Monday I was speaking with him. On Tuesday he was delirious, on Wednesday dead. To the last he talked to me about our opera. It seems like a dream to me. The most honest soul and the most faithful friend! I wish I were lying there, in his place. For he leaves the world with fame!" (SDB 824).

The obituaries in the Viennese press seem to note more the passing of a beloved figure than that of a great artist – they comment repeatedly on Schubert's simplicity, shyness, modesty, and industriousness. "He lived solely for art and for a small circle of friends," reported the *Wiener Allgemeine Theaterzeitung* (SMF 10). Franz von Schlechta, an acquaintance since Schubert's Seminary days, published a short poem in the *Wiener Zeitschrift für Kunst*, which began, "The Muses weep, one favorite joins another [i.e. Beethoven]: Wherefore thou too, so young, so full of hope?" (SDB 838).

Over the course of the next year, some of Schubert's closest friends and supporters wrote poems and extended memorial essays. Their reminiscences provide valuable insights. Although the myth-making about Schubert began immediately after his death (legends about Beethoven had already circulated widely during his lifetime), the first tributes nonetheless offer a more immediate, honest, and restrained view of his life, career, and music than those that would emerge years later, sometimes from the very same writers. Appropriately, Spaun produced a long and penetrating account, which amounted to a miniature biography.[2] Sonnleithner, Mayrhofer, and Bauernfeld contributed essays to various Viennese journals. Ferdinand Schubert apparently wrote his tribute around this time as well, although it remained unpublished until Schumann printed it in 1839.

Other close friends, such as Kupelwieser and Schwind, did not write anything at the time and later discouraged biographers' inquiries. Notably absent is any word from Schober, who decades later still had not put anything on paper. In 1869, he told Bauernfeld sadly that he had often tried unsuccessfully to "write a little book about [Schubert] and our life together . . . How can I make clear to you the insuperable inability to write? How make clear to you, who write so easily and so excellently, the inability which has pursued me to the point of desperation throughout my life and which, as a matter of fact, is the cause of unhappiness in me?" (SMF 205). While friends and acquaintances recorded their memories, no objective observer thought to write a biography, and therefore memories that might have been more accurately preserved in 1830s and early 1840s are lost to history. Only years later, and at a point when Schubert's stature had already increased enormously, did potential biographers begin to solicit material – too late, one might say. Alois Fuchs and Ferdinand Luib assembled information, as did Franz Liszt, for unrealized biographical projects. Eventually Heinrich Kreissle von Hellborn used this material for the first substantial biography.

By the time Kreissle's biography finally appeared in the mid 1860s, considerable interest in Schubert the man had developed because so much more of his music was at last available. After his death at thirty-one, Schubert's career had flourished. The pre-eminent Viennese critic Eduard Hanslick succinctly captured Schubert's unusual posthumous productivity in the remark that opened this chapter – Schubert seemed to be "composing invisibly" (SMF 383). The continual flow of new masterpieces even raised occasional speculation that not all these works were authentic: "All Paris has been in a state of amazement at the posthumous diligence of the song-writer Franz Schubert," commented *The Musical World* in 1839, "who, while one would think his ashes repose in peace in Vienna, is still making eternal new songs, and putting drawing-rooms in commotion."[3]

In fact, with rare exceptions, the dazzling "new" compositions were indeed authentic. While nearly 190 of Schubert's songs were published during his lifetime (an extremely large number in comparison with other composers, and a quantity supplemented by widely circulated handwritten copies), they did not account for even a third of his complete Lied output. The bulk of Schubert's manuscripts went to Ferdinand, who sought their publication. During the 1830s and 1840s, Diabelli released 137 Lieder for the first time, and the Parisian publisher Simon Richault expanded Schubert's foreign renown by issuing more than 300 in French translation.

If one has to choose, as Schubert had to, which are his most valuable songs, the vast majority appear among those printed in the 1820s. In other words, Schubert's contemporaries knew his greatest songs, whereas those that surfaced posthumously, though they include many marvels, are often of lesser worth. Such was not the case, however, with Schubert's instrumental music, which explains why the discovery of so much astonished so many. The Piano Sonata in A Minor (D664), the "Trout" Quintet (D667), and the "Death and the Maiden" Quartet (D810) appeared shortly after Schubert's death. Diabelli published the Piano Trio in B-flat, Op. 99 (D898) in 1836 and the Sonata in C, the "Grand Duo" (D812), dedicating it to Clara Wieck, in 1837. By the end of the decade Diabelli had released the final three piano sonatas (D958–60). As Schubert's intended dedicatee, Hummel, had died in the meantime, the publisher decided to honor Robert Schumann, an appropriate recognition of all his service to Schubert.

The dissemination of Schubert's music benefited enormously from the efforts of a select group of passionately supportive performers and composers. Anna Milder's important farewell concerts in 1835–36 included not only Schubert songs but also the E-flat Piano

Trio (D929). Beginning in the 1850s, the Hellmesberger Quartet premiered such string masterpieces as the G Major Quartet (D887) and
the C Major Quintet (D956), which led to their publication, together
with the Octet (D803). Vogl continued to sing in private concerts until
his death in 1840, on the twelfth anniversary of Schubert's death. The
appearance of Lieder on mixed programs, semi-private concerts, and
Schubertiades gradually expanded into more formal *Liederabende*, reci-
tals, and symphonic concerts; Schubert Lieder were in fact largely
responsible for the shift in the genre from the private to the public
sphere. Julius Stockhausen's innovative concerts in the 1850s, especially those in which he featured the Müller song cycles, marked an
important transition to the Lied recital as we know it today. (Clara
Schumann and Brahms were his preferred accompanists.) Even dramatic works received limited exposure. At Schober's urging, Liszt
conducted the première of *Alfonso und Estrella* in Weimar in 1854, *Die
Verschworenen* was given a concert performance in Vienna in 1861 (and
staged in Frankfurt later that season), and the unfinished cantata
Lazarus was presented in 1863.

The premières of Schubert's symphonies provided the greatest
impetus for his elevation in stature to a more serious and universal
composer. None had been performed publicly during his lifetime,
although Schubert had heard all the completed ones in private or conservatory settings. While the Sixth, the "Little" C Major (D589), was
performed just four weeks after his death, the first three symphonies,
which today are played rather frequently, had to wait until the late
1870s and 1880s, when Sir August Manns gave their first performances in England. After learning of the "Great" C Major Symphony
(D944) during a visit to Vienna, Schumann encouraged his friend
Mendelssohn to present the work in Leipzig in 1839. Schumann then
wrote up the piece in a famous critical essay – the occasion of his
remark on its "heavenly length."[4] Then finally, more than forty years
after its composition, the conductor Johann Herbeck presented the
"Unfinished" Symphony on 17 December 1865 at the Gesellschaft
der Musikfreunde. While Hanslick had previously warned of "over-

zealous Schubert worship and adulation of Schubert relics," he now hailed this work and its performance, which "excited extraordinary enthusiasm" and "brought new life into our concert halls."[5]

In short, during the decades following his death, many of Schubert's supreme works at last saw the light of day. Indeed, it was only with the publication of the first collected Schubert edition that performers, critics, and audiences had easy access to complete works. The famous Leipzig firm of Breitkopf & Härtel, which in 1816 had rejected *Erlkönig*, undertook this ambitious project in 1884; funded largely by the admiring Schubert patron Nicholas Dumba, it was commendably edited by Eusebius Mandyczewski, archivist of the Gesellschaft der Musikfreunde, along with Brahms, Hellmesberger, and the pianist Julius Epstein, among others. The thirty-nine folio volumes were completed in time for the centennial celebrations of Schubert's birth in 1897.[6]

While the gradual emergence of great unknown compositions surprised and delighted many, there were larger and more profound consequences as well. The meaning of "Schubert" kept on evolving, not simply as part of an expected and normal reassessment of a known body of works, but because that corpus and its context constantly shifted. Schumann had once lamented that Schubert did not live long enough to give the world a "Beethoven Tenth." Some years later, after discovering the C Major Symphony, he realized that in fact Schubert had written such a work. He argued that one who "is not yet acquainted with this symphony knows very little about Schubert" and urged that unpublished compositions be immediately released so that "the world finally arrives at the full appreciation of Schubert."[7] The irony is that Schumann himself never heard, or even knew the existence of, the "Unfinished" Symphony, which was only unveiled a decade after his death.

Ferdinand Schubert, friends, publishers, critics, and biographers all played crucial roles in advancing Schubert's fame after his death, and it is understandable that some of them had self-interested reasons. (Ferdinand, for one, had more than twenty children from two marriages and constantly needed money.) The foremost advocacy of Schubert, however, came from great composers. If the devotion and support of Schumann, Liszt, and Brahms may have been partly self-serving, it was primarily in the artistic sense that these composers learned from their encounters with Schubert's music.[8]

While everyone acknowledges Beethoven's enormous influence on later composers, we tend to forget, or minimize, other potent forces such as Schubert. In 1828 the eighteen-year-old Schumann had written two "fan" letters to Schubert, which he never sent. Upon hearing of Schubert's death Schumann cried all night, and a decade later made his pilgrimage to Vienna, during which he discovered the C Major Symphony. He visited Währing Cemetery and "gazed long on those two sacred graves, almost envying the person buried between them – a certain Count O'Donnell, if I am not mistaken."[9] Clara Wieck had already made a similar excursion to Vienna, prompting a special request from her future husband: "Will you not pay a visit to our beloved Schubert and Beethoven? Take with you some sprigs of myrtle, twine them together in twos, and lay them on the graves. Whisper your name and mine as you do so – not a word besides. You understand?"

Schumann's criticism marked an interpretive high point in Schubert's reception. He recognized, valued, and extolled Schubert's genius as had no other composer or critic; he repeatedly paired him with Beethoven and asserted that his music initiated a new era of Romanticism. And in contrast to the kind of attention Schubert had predominantly received elsewhere, Schumann probed the keyboard and instrumental music, only rarely commenting on the Lieder. His considerable efforts to get works known, and his ardent praise in the prestigious journal he helped establish and edit, the *Neue Zeitschrift für Musik*, mightily helped to advance Schubert's reputation.

Liszt's advocacy took many different forms. It is not known for certain whether he had met Schubert, although they were both living in Vienna during the years Liszt studied with Czerny and Salieri (1821–23). Liszt and Schubert seem an odd pair. A number of important if obvious features are at odds: lifespan, nationality, social stat-ure, public recognition, performing abilities, and compositional style; and yet as pianist, conductor, arranger, editor, and essayist Liszt was perhaps the central figure in the nineteenth-century promotion of Schubert. He frequently gave audiences their first exposure to his music, performing it in countless concerts throughout Europe during the late 1830s and 1840s. Liszt's many reworkings of Schubert's com-positions are lasting evidence of his devotion. He arranged for piano some fifty-six songs, marvelously inventive adaptations that range from fairly faithful transcriptions to structurally diffuse fantasies. Despite the awesome difficulty many of them posed, publishers could barely keep up with public demand. Liszt also arranged many marches and dances, all of which figured prominently in his concert repertoire. His largest project was an orchestration of the "Wanderer" Fantasy, which provides the closest thing we have to a Schubert piano concerto.

Liszt's activities in reworking Schubert's music highlight the unusual importance that arrangements played in the growth of Schubert's fame. Typically, the process worked the other way. As with recordings today, the most famous and popular pieces tended to receive principal attention from arrangers, and for that reason pub-lishers' catalogues throughout the century bulged with all manner of reworkings to suit nearly every conceivable combination of instru-ments. Schubert, in contrast to a popular figure like Rossini, was often arranged, at least at first, because the nature of the musical material proved so conducive (after all, Schubert "arranged" his own music when he incorporated songs into larger instrumental works). An extraordinarily famous work such as Erlkönig was reworked more than a hundred times during the nineteenth century, but so were countless less familiar songs, dances, and other compositions.[10] That Liszt, the premier virtuoso of the day, would play Schubert's music, mainly in some sort of arrangement, on most of his concerts helped immeasurably to spread Schubert's name across Europe and beyond.

Brahms too expressed a passionate and enduring devotion to

Schubert's music in a variety of ways – performances, editions, and arrangements. He quoted Schubert melodies in a number of works, edited the symphonies and other pieces, arranged dances, and orchestrated Lieder. In the early 1860s, Brahms visited Vienna and wrote to a friend that the city was filled with "the sacred memory of the great musicians whose lives and work are brought daily to our minds. In the case of Schubert especially, one has the impression of his being still alive. Again and again one meets people who talk of him as a good friend, again and again one comes across new works, the existence of which was unknown."[11] Brahms worried greatly about the safety of such manuscripts that existed without copies, and he proved instrumental in getting some of them published. (On the other hand, some early pieces ultimately disappeared because Brahms objected so strenuously to their inclusion in the first collected edition.)

This is not the place to trace completely Schubert's afterlife in memory, publication, performance, and legend. As some of the highlights just sketched show, his "career" continued to advance throughout the century. At the same time as musicians, biographers, and critics were assembling a more truly representative picture of his musical achievement, Schubert the man entered public consciousness on a more popular level. The trappings of immortality came slowly at first but built to a high pitch between the time of the Schubert centenary celebrations in 1897 and 1928. Many activities were initiated by the Wiener Männergesang-Verein (founded in 1843) and the Wiener Schubertbund (founded in 1863), which helped place plaques on nearly every building where Schubert lived, organized Schubert exhibitions and museums, and presented innumerable Schubert concerts and festivals. Schubert's time had already clearly come by 1872, when his statue, the first in Vienna honoring a composer, was erected in the city park.

I have suggested not only that Beethoven's death profoundly affected Schubert's final twenty months, but also that Schubert's own early death indelibly marks his image. The presence of death, which per-

20 The Schubert Monument by Karl Kundmann in Vienna's Stadtpark (1872).

vades so much of Schubert's music, haunts his reception as well. The
poetic justice of Schubert's grave being so close to Beethoven's reso-
nated throughout the nineteenth century, during which time the significance and deeper meaning of Grillparzer's funeral oration for
Beethoven and his epitaph for Schubert became fully revealed. By the

1860s, the cemetery in Währing had fallen into some disrepair, and as part of a restoration project the bodies of Schubert and Beethoven were exhumed. Their remains were submitted to a scientific process that measured, studied, and compared their skulls so as better to understand the mechanisms of genius; they were then reburied in more secure metal coffins.[12]

For the music historian concerned with Schubert's changing image, it is significant that by this time his reputation had risen so far that so much fuss could be made. Moreover, the discussion and honoring of Schubert continued to be relative to, and even to have direct connections with, Beethoven. The comparison of these musical geniuses by way of quack phrenology is only part of Schubert's deathly elevation to Beethoven's side. Kreissle wrote in 1864:

> Nowadays, when the greater part of Schubert's treasures has been revealed to us, Grillparzer's epitaph, which gave offense so many years ago, sounds to our ears still more strangely, and we may hope that over Schubert's future resting place there will be nothing carved but the name of the composer. As does the simple "Beethoven" over that great man's grave, the word "Schubert" will speak volumes.[13]

This remark was fulfilled some years later when Währing Cemetery was deconsecrated. The former cemetery eventually became a Schubert Park where children play today oblivious to the history of the location. The original monuments to Beethoven and Schubert are still there to visit, but in 1888 their bodies were transferred in two solemn ceremonies to the "Grove of Honor" in Vienna's new Central Cemetery, where, as Kreissle had hoped, the final tombstone simply reads "Franz Schubert."

What further masterpieces might Schubert have created? The question may be sentimental, but not pointless. It has been asked too often to be simply dismissed out of hand. The continued pursuit of unfinished and lost works by Schubert, the recurring fantasies of more treasures, has after all proved not so fantastic. As the nineteenth century gradually discovered, and as anyone who studies the totality of his oeuvre eventually learns, Schubert fulfilled much of the "far fairer hopes" of which his contemporaries could only dream.

Who gives us another Eroica?
Who fresh Miller songs?
The reign of glorious Music
is over and shall not return.   Eduard von Bauernfeld 1828

Epilogue: Schubert today

Josef von Spaun's lament in the 1860s that the first biography of his dear friend contained "too little light and too much shadow" might be echoed regarding every narrative account of Schubert's life that has appeared during the intervening century and a half. (Otto Erich Deutsch's "objective" collections of documents prove the exception.) Reasons why Schubert remains elusive, beginning with the simple lack of documentation and extending to the belated discovery of so many compositions, have been touched on in the preceding chapters. While biographers may be frustrated by Schubert's supposedly event-less existence, that has certainly not discouraged novelists, operetta composers, and film-makers from turning its raw material into poig-nant fantasy. Certainly the absence of a compelling life narrative and of a multidimensional character has precisely encouraged such fictive appropriations. Much of the public still dearly embraces the bitter-sweet, distorted, and trivial image created long ago.

I am continually surprised at how confidently some people make assertions about Schubert's personality, as if they harbored secret, privileged information. His friends often referred to "our Schubert," and a comparable possessiveness remains to this day among those who never, of course, met the man. Love of Schubert's music triggers this proprietary and protective attitude; so too, perhaps, does the fear that acknowledging repressed forces in his life might in some way reflect on the loving listener as well. The unusually intimate nature of music deepens such an engagement. One reason why the representation of Schubert in operettas and movies has been so successful, as well as insidiously seductive, is the abundant presence of his own compositions. The aura of authenticity drawn from his art, no matter how mangled the music usually becomes when put on stage or screen, transcends the banality of the life story being offered.

The astonishing emotional and generic range of Schubert's music, the lack of documentary evidence, and conflicting reports about his personality all help to sustain a wide variety of images. Such malleability brings to our attention the fact that changing perceptions always reflect changing times – a phenomenon remarkably revealed in the language used to describe Schubert. A wonderful example is the recent revisionist arguments about Schubert's personality. Thanks to a historical irony, the revisionists find themselves caught up in a double-play on the word "gay," arguing that Schubert simultaneously was gay (i.e. homosexual) and that he was not gay (i.e. merry). The same connotations do not exist in the German language, and would not in any case apply to Schubert's time. A hundred years ago the culture that produced *Das Dreimäderlhaus* and similar trivializing fare most enjoyed Schubert's sunny and bittersweet creations. The "Trout" Quintet, *Ave Maria*, the military marches, and other pieces in that vein seemed perfectly to complement a cheap and phony life story. Throughout the English translations of the standard Schubert documents we find references to the "gay Schubert," "the company of his gay friends," to their "gay times" and "gay existence." German words such as *lustig* and *fröhlich* (meaning "merry," "cheerful," or "happy") were consistently translated as "gay" in the 1946 and 1958 English translations of the documents collected by Deutsch, as well as in books based on those fundamental compilations.

By the end of the twentieth century, after two World Wars and other horrors, the music of a more complex Schubert is most representative. The late chamber music and piano sonatas, *Winterreise*, and the Heine Lieder today hold the highest esteem. At the same time, a more honest consideration of the historical evidence has taken seriously reports that were before psychologically, if not literally, repressed: Schubert had a "dual nature," he possessed "a black-winged demon of sorrow and melancholy," he drank excessively on occasion, he was a "hedonist" who indulged in "sensual living." By now, the idea of a gay Schubert has taken on a very different meaning and prompted fierce debates.

The issue of Schubert's sexuality is far from resolved, not only because of the slippery nature of the evidence involved, but also because the terms of what is being discussed are not yet clear. The largely homosocial extent of Schubert's life – unremarkable in his time – is beyond doubt, but not the forms its emotional and physical expression may have taken. I find it unlikely that most members of the so-called Schubert Circle were either lovers amongst themselves or with male prostitutes. And yet Schubert, and perhaps some others, may very well have been predominantly homosexual or bisexual in their libidinal object choices, no matter how, when, where, and with whom these desires found release. More work will have to be done before we know enough about the social and sexual practices of the time in Vienna, particularly of the men and women in Schubert's orbit.

And while this issue is indisputably of considerable interest, it does not seem to me to warrant – purely on biographical and musical grounds relating to Schubert – the inordinate attention it has received in North America. (At the major European conferences held during the Schubert Bicentennial in 1997, the matter continued to be avoided – especially in Vienna, where the topic was exactly "Schubert and His Friends.") Just as some of the arguments about Schubert's sexuality have bordered on, or crossed into, the homophobic, so too a good deal of the speculation and self-indulgent special pleading for his gayness has displayed a remarkable lack of knowledge, insight, and nuance. Schubert has become the screen onto which ever-changing agendas are still being projected. For some, who summarily reject the very prospect of Schubert's homosexuality, the aim is to uphold the purity of a great German composer and to make certain that this icon of innocence remains forever unsullied. For others, the goal often is to act out an identity politics that, no matter how attractive as a political agenda for the turn of the millennium, risks doing considerable historical disservice to Schubert's own time.

Schubert's popular image in Europe recently found compelling, if again distorting, expression in Fritz Lehner's film *Mit meinen heissen Tränen* (1986), which also introduced a darker Schubert – not simply suffering, but ill, alienated, and isolated even among family and friends. One can only marvel at how Schubert and his music have generated so many interpretations and accommodated such a variety of appropriations over time; Schubert has, after all, been put to various political and ideological uses in the past. While we may be tempted only to lament this fact, to regret that we know so little and can therefore need to make up so much, we might rather celebrate the range and emotional depth that Schubert's art encompasses, music that evokes such a breadth of responses and interpretations and that gives such diverse feelings of pain and pleasure.

NOTES

1 Representing Schubert: "A life devoted to art"

1 I have explored the construction of Schubert's image at greater length in "'Poor Schubert': Images and Legends of the Composer," in The Cambridge Companion to Schubert, ed. Christopher H. Gibbs (Cambridge, 1997) [henceforth Companion to Schubert], 36–55; some brief passages of this and later chapters adapt material from the Companion.

2 Heinrich Kreissle von Hellborn, Franz Schubert (Vienna, 1865), translated by Arthur Duke Coleridge, The Life of Franz Schubert (London, 1869; rpt. New York, 1972) [henceforth Kreissle, Life], II: 169–70.

3 The standard iconographical sources for Schubert are: Otto Erich Deutsch, Sein Leben in Bildern (Munich and Leipzig, 1913); Ernst Hilmar and Otto Brusatti, Franz Schubert: Ausstellung der Wiener Stadt- und Landesbibliothek zum 150. Todestag des Komponisten (Vienna, 1978); Ernst Hilmar, Schubert (Graz, 1990); and the exhibition catalogue Schubert 200 Jahre, ed. Ilija Dürhammer and Gerrit Waidelich (Heidelberg, 1997).

4 Otto Biba suggests that Schubert is singing with Josefine Fröhlich and Johann Michael Vogl, although I rather doubt the male singer is the latter; see "Einige neue und wichtige Schubertiana im Archiv der Gesellschaft der Musikfreunde," Österreichische Musikzeitschrift 33 (1978), 604–05.

5 John M. Gingerich, "Schubert's Beethoven Project: The Chamber Music, 1824–1828" (PhD diss., Yale University, 1996).
6 Maurice J. E. Brown, *Essays on Schubert* (London, 1966), 161; his suggestion that Vogl and Schubert are performing *An die Musik*, mentioned below, is on page 164.
7 Rita Steblin, *Ein unbekanntes frühes Schubert-Porträt? Franz Schubert und der Maler Josef Abel* (Tutzing, 1992). The portrait is included in *The Romantic Era*, vol. 2 of the *Heritage of Music*, ed. Michael Raeburn and Alan Kendall (Oxford, 1989), 74; and in Yehudi Menuhin and Curtis W. Davis, *The Music of Man* (New York, 1979), 157, as well as in many other places.

2 Young Schubert: "The master in the boy"

1 The most reliable information about Schubert's early years and his family genealogy is found in Herwig Knaus, *Franz Schubert: Vom Vorstadtkind zum Compositeur* (Vienna, 1997) and Heinz Schöny, "Franz Schubert: Herkunft und Verwandtschaft," *Jahrbuch der Heraldisch-Genealogischen Gesellschaft* 3.9 (1974/78), 1–26; information about Schubert's father is drawn from Otto Erich Deutsch, "Schuberts Vater," in *Alt-Wiener Kalender 1924*, ed. Alois Trost (Vienna, 1924), 134–48.
2 This document is not in SDB; a facsimile is given in *Schubert 200 Jahre*, ed. Ilija Dürhammer and Gerrit Waidelich (Heidelberg, 1997), 66.
3 The information about Schubert's education is drawn from David Gramit, "The Intellectual and Aesthetic Tenets of Franz Schubert's Circle" (PhD diss., Duke University, 1987) [henceforth Gramit, "Schubert's Circle"]; and Ilija Dürhammer, "Schuberts literarische Heimat: Dichtung und Literaturrezeption der Schubert-Freunde" (PhD diss., Universität Wien, 1998).
4 The first edition of Deutsch's catalogue appeared in English and has recently been reissued by Dover Publications; the German edition is updated and much more detailed; *Schubert: Thematic Catalogue of all his Works* (1951; rpt. New York, 1995); *Franz Schubert: Thematisches Verzeichnis seiner Werke in chronologischer Folge* (Kassel, 1978).

5 The number of works is somewhat misleading as many Lieder, partsongs, and dances were written or published in sets. Songs such as Erlkönig and Gretchen am Spinnrade therefore count as separate works, whereas Schwanengesang, which groups thirteen songs, likewise gets a single Deutsch number (D957). If every individual vocal work and dance were counted separately, the total number would be much higher.

6 Quoted in Leon Botstein, "History, Rhetoric, and the Self: Robert Schumann and Music Making in German-Speaking Europe, 1800–1860" in Schumann and his World, ed. R. Larry Todd (Princeton, 1994), 10.

7 Schering, Franz Schuberts Symphonie in h-moll und ihr Geheimnis (Würzburg, 1939); Maurice Brown, Schubert: A Critical Biography (New York, 1958), 114–16; for further literature, see the bibliography listed in Schubert Lexikon, ed. Ernst Hilmar and Margret Jestremski (Graz, 1997), 296–97.

8 Kreissle, Life, 1: 35.

9 See Maurice J. E. Brown, "The Therese Grob Collection of Songs by Schubert," Music and Letters (1968), 122–34.

10 Rita Steblin, "Franz Schubert und das Ehe-Consens Gesetz von 1815," Schubert durch die Brille 9 (June 1992), 32–42.

3 Ingenious Schubert: "The prince of song"

1 On Music and Musicians, trans. Paul Rosenfeld (New York, 1946) [henceforth On Music], 242–43.

2 For an overview of the poets Schubert set see Susan Youens, "Schubert's Poets" in Companion to Schubert, 99–117; and John Reed, The Schubert Song Companion (Manchester, 1985).

3 Gramit, "Schubert's Circle."

4 David Gramit, "'The Passion for Friendship': Music, Cultivation, and Identity in Schubert's Circle," in Companion to Schubert, 61–62.

5 Die Unsinnsgesellschaft: Franz Schubert, Leopold Kupelwieser und ihr Freundeskreis (Vienna, 1998).

6 Information on Schubert's religious music is drawn from Hans Jaskulsky's book, Die lateinischen Messen Franz Schuberts (Mainz, 1986).

4 Popular Schubert: "The turning point"

1 See Brian Newbould, "A Schubert Palindrome," 19th-Century Music 15 (Spring 1992), 207–14; Schubert: The Music and the Man (Berkeley, 1997); "Schubert im Spiegel," Musiktheorie 13 (1998), 101–10.
2 Gramit, "Schubert's Circle," 156.
3 For a list of places Schubert lived, see SDB 929–31, as well as Rudolf Klein, Schubert Stätten (Vienna, 1972).
4 Walburga Litschauer, Neue Dokumente zum Schubert-Kreis, 2 vols. (Vienna, 1986, 1993) [henceforth Litschauer, Dokumente] I: 52.
5 The most thorough study of Schubert's dramatic music is Elizabeth Norman McKay, Franz Schubert's Music for the Theater (Tutzing, 1991).
6 About the Society, see Richard von Perger and Robert Hirschfeld, Geschichte der k.k. Gesellschaft der Musikfreunde in Wien (Vienna, 1912). Schubert's connection with the Society is examined in three articles by Otto Biba, "Franz Schubert und die Gesellschaft der Musikfreunde in Wien," in Schubert-Kongress Wien 1978: Bericht, ed. Otto Brusatti (Graz, 1979), 23–36; "Franz Schubert in den musikalischen Abendunterhaltungen der Gesellschaft der Musikfreunde," in Schubert-Studien: Festgabe der Oesterreichischen Akademie der Wissenschaften zum Schubert-Jahr 1978, ed. Franz Grasberger and Othmar Wessely (Vienna, 1978), 7–31; and "Schubert's Position in Viennese Musical Life," 19th-Century Music 3 (November 1979), 106–13.
7 For a longer discussion of this significant event and its immediate consequences, as well as the sources for these and other reviews, see Christopher H. Gibbs, "The Presence of Erlkönig: Reception and Reworkings of a Schubert Lied" (PhD diss., Columbia University, 1992), 58–64.
8 Franz Schubert: Jahre der Krise 1818–1823, ed. Werner Aderhold, Walther Dürr, and Walburga Litschauer (Kassel, 1985).
9 Brian Newbould, Schubert and the Symphony (London, 1992).
10 "Schubert's 'Unfinished' Symphony," 19th-Century Music 21 (Fall 1997), 111–33.

5 Dark Schubert: "A black-winged demon of sorrow and melancholy"

1 Information about Schubert's health is drawn from Eric Sams, "Schubert's Illness Re-examined," Musical Times 121 (1980), 15–22; Anton Neumayr, Music and Medicine: Haydn, Mozart, Beethoven, and Schubert, trans. Bruce Cooper Clarke (Bloomington, 1994), 347–413; and Hans D. Kiemle, "Woran starb Schubert eigentlich? Ein Beitrag aus toxikologischer Sicht," in Schubert durch die Brille 16/17 (January 1996), 41–51.

2 SDB 476; this is Joshua Rifkin's revised translation, which appears in his as yet unpublished paper "Schubert's Sexuality: Some Questions of Language and Logic." I am grateful to the author for sharing his essay with me.

3 Franz Schubert: A Biography (Oxford, 1996) [henceforth McKay, Schubert], 133–63.

4 McKay, Schubert, 125–27; 155–56.

5 Gramit, "Schubert's Circle," 388; translation modified from Maynard Solomon, "Schubert: Some Consequences of Nostalgia," 19th-Century Music 17 (Summer 1993), 38.

6 This idea is explored in two articles by Hugh Macdonald, "Schubert's Volcanic Temper," Musical Times 119 (1978), 949–52; and "Schubert's Pendulum," Schubert durch die Brille 21 (June 1998), 143–51.

7 Schubert, Müller, and Die schöne Müllerin (Cambridge, 1997).

8 Schubert, 110.

6 Poor Schubert: "Miserable reality"

1 Peter Clive, Schubert and his World: A Biographical Dictionary (Oxford, 1997), 191.

2 Donald W. MacArdle, "Beethoven and Schuppanzigh," Music Review 26 (1965), 3–14.

3 Musical connections among Schubert's works are examined by John Reed in The Schubert Song Companion (Manchester, 1985), 494–98; see also Maurice Brown, "Schubert: Instrumental Derivations in the Songs," Music and Letters 28 (1947), 207–15; and Reinhard van Hoorickx, "Schubert's Reminiscences of his Own Works" Musical Quarterly 60 (1974), 373–88.

4 There has been relatively little study of Schubert's critical reception; see Herbert Biehle, *Schuberts Lieder: In Kritik und Literatur* (Berlin, 1928); Christoph-Hellmut Mahling, "Zur Rezeption von Werken Franz Schuberts," in *Zur Aufführungspraxis der Werke Franz Schuberts*, ed. Vera Schwarz (Munich, 1981), 12–33; Otto Brusatti, *Schubert im Wiener Vormärz* (Graz, 1978); and Part III "Reception" in *Companion to Schubert*.

5 *On Music*, 116.

6 The redating of this work is treated in John Reed, *Schubert: The Final Years* (New York, 1972); and Robert S. Winter, "Paper Studies and the Future of Schubert Research," in *Schubert Studies: Problems of Style and Chronology*, ed. Eva Badura-Skoda and Peter Branscombe (Cambridge, 1982), 209–75.

7 Solomon first raised the issue in "Franz Schubert's 'Mein Traum'," *American Imago* 38 (1981), 137–54. His case only achieved wide notoriety with public lectures and the article "Franz Schubert and the Peacocks of Benvenuto Cellini," *19th-Century Music* 12 (Spring 1989), 193–206; see also "Schubert: Music, Sexuality, Culture," a special issue of *19th-Century Music* 17 (Summer 1993). This quote is taken from the 1993 article, page 35.

7 *Late Schubert: "Who shall stand beside Beethoven?"*

1 Kreissle, *Schubert*, 1: 268. Maynard Solomon, after a careful review of the published literature, has concluded that their encounters were "fleeting"; "Schubert and Beethoven," *19th-Century Music* 3 (November 1979), 114–25.

2 This passage, and some of the following quotations of material dealing with Beethoven, are taken from *Thayer's Life of Beethoven*, rev. and ed. by Elliot Forbes (Princeton, 1967), 1053–54. Grillparzer's oration, which exists in a number of variants, appears on pages 1057–58 (I have modified the translation).

3 *Geschichte der europäisch-abendländischen oder unserer heutigen Musik* (Leipzig, 1834); cf. Eduard Hanslick's *Geschichte des Concertwesens in Wien* (Vienna, 1869), 139ff.

4 Litschauer, *Dokumente*, 1: 61, 67.

5 Litschauer, *Dokumente*, 1: 68

6 Rita Steblin, "Schubert's Relationship with Women: An Historical Account," in *Schubert Studies*, ed. Brian Newbould (Aldershot, 1998), 220–43.

7 The letters relating most directly to Schubert are generally in SDB; many among other members of the circle are in Litschauer, *Dokumente*, and the dissertations by Gramit and Dürhammer cited in note 2 to chapter 3.

8 I have explored the "secret program" of the trio in program notes for the 1997 Schubertiade at the 92nd Street Y in New York City, and the Schubert Festival at Carnegie Hall (5 May 1997); a more in-depth study is forthcoming. For information about the Swedish folksong, see Manfred Willfort, "Das Urbild des Andante aus Schuberts Klaviertrio Es-Dur, D 929" *Österreichische Musikzeitschrift* 33 (1978), 277–83.

9 "Schubert's 'Auf dem Strom'," in *Schubert Studies: Problems of Style and Chronology*, ed. Eva Badura-Skoda and Peter Branscombe (Cambridge, 1982), 25–46.

10 *On Music*, 118–20.

11 *Wiener-Zeitung* 67 (23 March 1829), 304.

12 Litschauer, *Dokumente*, II: 104.

13 *Der Sammler*, 23 (21 February 1829), 92.

14 For a discussion of Schubert's final illness see Sams (cited in note 1, chapter 5), and McKay, *Schubert*, 324; 329–30.

8 *Immortal Schubert: "Composing invisibly"*

1 *On Music*, 118.

2 Anton Ottenwalt, Spaun's brother-in-law, abridged the long piece, which appeared anonymously in three installments of the Linz periodical *Österreichisches Bürgerblatt für Verstand, Herz und gute Laune*. For the original version, see *Erinnerungen an Schubert: Josef von Spauns erste Lebensbeschreibung*, ed. Georg Schünemann (Berlin and Zurich, 1936), which is partly translated in SMF 18–29.

3 Quoted by Otto Erich Deutsch in "The Reception of Schubert's Works in England," *Monthly Musical Record* 81 (1951), 202.

4 *On Music*, 107–12.

5 *Hanslick's Musical Criticisms*, ed. and trans. Henry Pleasants (New York, 1978), 102.

6 Otto Erich Deutsch, "Schubert: The Collected Works," *Music and Letters* 32 (1951), 226–34.

7 *On Music*, 108, and SMF 405.

8 Information about these composers' connections to Schubert is drawn from Marie Luise Maintz, *Franz Schubert in der Rezeption Robert Schumanns* (Kassel, 1995); Thomas Kabisch, *Liszt und Schubert* (Munich, 1984); and Robert Pascall, "Brahms and Schubert," *Musical Times* 124 (1983), 289; "'My Love of Schubert – No Fleeting Fancy': Brahms's Response to Schubert," *Schubert durch die Brille* 21 (June 1998), 39–60.

9 *On Music*, 107. The following letter is in *Robert und Clara Schumann: Briefe einer Liebe*, Hanns-Josef Ortheil, ed. (Königstein, 1982), 79.

10 Reworkings of *Erlkönig* and of other compositions are examined in Christopher H. Gibbs, "The Presence of Erlkönig: Reception and Reworkings of a Schubert Lied" (PhD diss., Columbia University, 1992).

11 Cited in David Brodbeck, "Brahms's Edition of Twenty Schubert Ländler: An Essay in Criticism," in *Brahms Studies: Analytical and Historical Perspectives*, ed. George S. Bozarth (Oxford, 1990), 229.

12 The results are reported in *Actenmässige Darstellung der Ausgrabung und Wiederbeisetzung der irdischen Reste von Beethoven und Schubert* (Vienna, 1863); the second disinterment is described in a report of Vienna's Anthropological Society, see *Bericht über die am 22 September 1888 vorgenommene Untersuchung an den Gebeinen Franz Schuberts gelegentlich der Übertragung derselben von dem Währinger Orts-Friedhofe nach dem Central-Friedhofe der Stadt Wien* (Vienna, 1888).

13 Kreissle, *Schubert*, II: 150.

The foundation of all modern biographical work on Schubert is the two remarkable documentary volumes compiled and edited by Otto Erich Deutsch. *Schubert: A Documentary Biography* presents sources from the composer's lifetime in chronological order – from birth to death certificates, all known letters written by Schubert (as well as many letters to him), diary entries, reviews, and so forth. Some new materials have come to light in recent decades, and yet the collection is still quite complete. More progress has been made, however, in interpreting these sources and therefore Deutsch's helpful but often outdated commentary must be used with some caution. Deutsch also compiled all the reliable (or fairly reliable) reminiscences and memoirs about Schubert from those who knew him. *Schubert: Memoirs by his Friends* also includes his commentary. The German editions of these two volumes contain some additions and corrections. The International Franz Schubert Institute is in the process of issuing a new series of documents (the first volume appeared in 1993). The Institute publishes an invaluable journal, *Schubert durch die Brille*, which offers much of the latest Schubert scholarship. Articles are usually in German.

As these collections of documents, however useful and fascinating, are somewhat unwieldy and lack a narrative thread, many readers will want to consult other studies. Heinrich Kreissle von Hellborn's first substantial biography of Schubert appeared in a fairly complete

English translation in 1869 (reprinted in 1972) and is worth reading as the source of most later nineteenth-century information about Schubert. In the twentieth century, many popular English-language biographies of Schubert, often the ones most easily available in libraries and bookstores, are uncritical, poorly researched, and perpetuate questionable cliches. More responsible are the biographies by Maurice J. Brown, Schubert: A Critical Biography (New York, 1958) and John Reed, especially his Schubert: The Final Years (New York, 1972). The 1997 Schubert bicentennial prompted two up-to-date studies: Elizabeth Norman McKay's Franz Schubert: A Biography (Oxford, 1996) and Brian Newbould's Schubert: The Music and the Man (Berkeley, 1997). The former is the most detailed biographical treatment available in English, while the latter, as its title suggests, focuses on the music. The debates about Schubert's sexuality have taken place largely in the journal 19th-Century Music, especially volumes 12 (1989), 17 (1993) and 22 (1998).

Among the surveys of Schubert's music are Alfred Einstein's opinionated but often insightful Schubert: A Musical Portrait (New York, 1951) and Franz Gal's Schubert and the Essence of Melody (London, 1974). Collections of essays worth consulting include Schubert: A Symposium, ed. Gerald Abraham (New York, 1947), and the more technical analytic studies in Schubert: Critical and Analytical Studies, ed. Walter Frisch (Lincoln and London, 1986). Each genre in which Schubert composed is given a chapter in The Cambridge Companion to Schubert, ed. Christopher H. Gibbs (Cambridge, 1997), and in the Schubert Handbuch, ed. Walther Dürr and Andreas Krause (Kassel, 1997).

Scholars have recently paid more attention to Schubert's milieu. Well worth consulting are Ernst Hilmar's Franz Schubert in his Time (Portland, 1988), and Schubert's Vienna, ed. Raymond Erickson (New Haven and London, 1997) which surveys the political, social, artistic, literary, theatrical, and musical culture of the time. The Cambridge Companion to Schubert contains essays by Christopher H. Gibbs, Leon Botstein, and David Gramit that examine Schubert's milieu and reception. Finally, Alice M. Hanson's *Musical Life in Biedermeier Vienna* (Cambridge, 1985) provides a fascinating view of Vienna's musical life.

Valuable reference works provide generally reliable information, and, even more usefully, include detailed bibliographic references that can help locate further information. As the number of notes in this present biography had to be kept to a minimum, I take solace in the knowledge that by consulting these volumes interested readers can track down more complete references on matters such as Schubert's health, his travels, individual genres and works, as well as on the complete cast of Schubert's friends, colleagues, poets, and so forth. The most comprehensive is the *Schubert Lexikon*, ed. Ernst Hilmar and Margret Jestremski (Graz, 1997; an updated and revised edition is forthcoming). Peter Clive's *Schubert and his World: A Biographical Dictionary* (Oxford, 1997) includes extended information on most in Schubert's circle, as well as on poets and others relevant figures. John Reed's *The Schubert Song Companion* (Manchester, 1985) presents an extended entry on every one of Schubert's songs.

Finally, Deutsch's catalogue of Schubert's compositions first appeared in English and has recently been reissued by Dover Publications; the German edition is much more detailed and up-to-date; *Schubert: Thematic Catalogue of all his Works* (1951; rpt. New York, 1995); *Franz Schubert: Thematisches Verzeichnis seiner Werke in chronologischer Folge* (Kassel, 1978). The first critical edition of Schubert's collected works, published by Breitkopf & Härtel (1884–97), was reissued by Dover Publications, New York, in 1965, and they have also released many inexpensive reprints of selected works. A new edition, the *Neue Schubert-Ausgabe*, is still in progress.